Also by Walid Phares

Future Jihad: Terrorist Strategies Against the West (2005)

The War of Ideas (2007)

The Confrontation (2008)

*The Coming Revolution: Struggle for
Freedom in the Middle East* (2010)

*The Lost Spring: U.S. Policy in the
Middle East and Catastrophes to Avoid* (2014)

*Iranian Regime, Regional Threats and
Strategic Responses* (2014)

To Senator Rick Scott

THE CHOICE

Trump vs. Obama-Biden in

U.S. Foreign Policy

Thank you for your service

Walid Phares

A POST HILL PRESS BOOK

ISBN: 978-1-64293-835-7
ISBN (eBook): 978-1-64293-836-4

The Choice:
Trump vs. Obama-Biden in U.S. Foreign Policy
© 2020 by Walid Phares
All Rights Reserved

Cover Design by Cody Corcoran

Post Hill Press
New York • Nashville
posthillpress.com

Published in the United States of America

TABLE OF CONTENTS

PROLOGUE

For too many years, Americans were told their country was facing threats, dangers, and complicated situations overseas that demanded U.S. commitment and, at times, blood and treasure. Since WWII, American families have paid the price of their country's constant involvement in conflicts abroad, and young men and women have consented to the ultimate sacrifice to keep the homeland safe and the United States' national security defended on national soil and worldwide. Foreign policy is one of the least understood areas of Washington practice and management among all other domestic and economic policies.

Most media, unfortunately, does not help our citizenry understand what is at stake in managing or mismanaging foreign policy. The price of failing to act properly or make the right decisions regarding our commitments overseas is paid dearly by the American public, as happened on September 11, 2001, and by Americans in many countries around the world, starting in Beirut in 1983, through East Africa in 1998 and Yemen in 2000, to the massacres of 9/11, and through today with hostages executed,

Americans jailed and tortured overseas, and the many victims of jihadi terror attacks in the homeland. Beyond the bloodshed, the U.S. economy can also suffer from a failed foreign policy. Dangerous agreements like the Iran deal of 2015 or the support to extremist Islamist movements and regimes have forced the United States to remain deployed and engaged militarily in the Greater Middle East, and reckless policies vis-à-vis Venezuela and North Korea could cost the American people dearly as well.

To avoid such catastrophes as those that have befallen America since the end of the Cold War, we need to constantly have a strategic, smart, relentless, and prescient foreign policy. Solid foreign policy is the only means by which to protect U.S. national security. Thus, the question is which camp can ensure such a policy for years to come—and on what principles?

Former president Barack Obama and his vice president, Joe Biden, led the country for eight years from 2009 to 2016. What did they do and how did they do in conducting foreign policy and maintaining our national security?

Joe Biden, who had been in politics for decades, was the vice president, supported Obama's decisions, oversaw them, and has them on his portfolio as he is running for president in 2020.

Donald Trump was never in politics before he ran for president but has been in presidential office—under attack the entire time—for four years.

No government and its bureaucracy is immune to mistakes,

wrong decisions, late decisions, and indecisions; that is a historical fact. But Americans have an obligation to choose one of the two directions mentioned above. November 2020—and its elections—will need aware citizens to make that choice. The next choice is vital.

This essay is to enlighten the American public and international public opinion about the choices we Americans have to make for the sake of this country—and the world. This essay is an effort to explain the foreign policy one can expect from either a re-elected President Trump administration or, if Joe Biden is elected, the foreign policy of, practically, a third Obama term.

CHAPTER 1

THERE IS A CHOICE

From the end of the Cold War to the attacks of September 11, 2001, to the so-called Arab Spring and the various other upheavals, wars, and conflicts spreading throughout the Greater Middle East and additional conflict zones in the world from Venezuela to North Korea, the American public has been confronted by a myriad of explanations and assertions, often contradictory. This is due in part to a media that has lost significant credibility because of its extreme partisanship instead of a focus on reliable information and has led to a point where average citizens are now either lost or unwilling to think for themselves in order to see clearly America's role in the world.

Americans, for example, are unsure whether the United States should stay in Afghanistan, Syria, and Iraq to fight the jihadists who were initially, and have been, responsible for the war against America since the 1990s—or withdraw all U.S. troops from battlefields around the world and instead allow the local governments and regional societies to handle those threats. Americans are unsure how to confront Iranian expansion and threats in the region and beyond. Americans are unsure whether the choice of Barack Obama to sign a deal with Iran was the right choice—or whether the decision by Donald Trump to withdraw from this agreement was a better choice.

Americans are confronted with conflicts happening thousands of miles away, such as those in Libya, in Yemen across the Gulf, in the Korean Peninsula, or closer to home in Venezuela—not to mention the wider consciousness regarding Russia and China.

What the public needs is a direction—or at least a standard of measurement against which citizens can understand these conflicts and their impact on U.S. national security—to allow them to compare the foreign policy agendas of sitting presidents to those of their opposition, so that they can make what they believe is the right choice every four years for president, or every two years or so for congressional representatives.

American and Western media have failed their audiences in terms of informing them about not just the facts on the ground overseas but also and mostly about the real positions that hostile forces and actors outside the country have been adopting regarding United States interests and national security. American academia has failed to prepare its students and ultimately the American public to understand the basics of geopolitics, making the vast majority of Americans unaware of how the world and global actors think about the United States and react to its policies. This tremendous gap created by the foreign policy establishment and media elite has caused and is continuing to cause tremendous damage to the capability of U.S. citizens to clearly see what is central to their safety, security, and future choices. The time is right—in fact there is now an urgency—for an informed testimony regarding foreign policy making and analysis, especially regarding developments since 9/11. There is a crossroads ahead that could affect the essence of who America is—and what she might become if her citizens are not provided with an accurate assessment of the threats and an analysis of possible future solutions.

America is heading towards historic elections for the presidency and Congress, elections which will determine any new foreign policy for at least the next four years and the decade to come. Americans must be honestly informed as to the challenges their country is facing as well as the threats that are developing both overseas and at home. Between 2016 and 2020 there have been many divisive debates between the opposition and the Trump administration on how to handle foreign policy and national security. Unfortunately, the U.S. media has extreme bias against Donald Trump and thus has not provided clear explanations about what America is truly facing overseas. The criticism that has been leveled against the administration has been focused solely on weakening and removing President Trump from office instead of providing a clear and accurate picture so that a real debate can actually take place among the citizens of this country.

American politics have become very divisive and have always been very personal. Instead of major ideas and concepts and even doctrinal views, generally the most popular and referred-to debates are in response to personalities, characters, and individual stories. Yet, global stability and national security should be framed in the best interests of the American public, not in the most expedient argument against a single candidate or official. As the United States is headed toward one of the most contentious election cycles in its history, Americans are facing (or should be confronted with) important questions as to how to conduct U.S. foreign policy and think in terms of national security.

Like any other government or any other administration, the Trump administration may have made mistakes in foreign policy and in national security policies, but the public needs to understand what those mistakes were and what was done to correct them, if anything. However, the most important thing for Americans to understand is the general strategic options that are available, which of those have been offered (whether they have been pursued or not), and which of those may be offered and/or pursued in the future.

The choice, however, will ultimately be a clear one: the options developed by the Trump administration—with all the mistakes and hesitations—or the options adopted by the Obama (and Biden) administration, which are embodied by the opposition today and thus could be part of future administrations depending on election results. Americans should be given a clear explanation of what the Trump administration's foreign policy doctrine has been, has evolved to, and could become in the future—given in clear contrast to the doctrines found in the Obama/Biden/Clinton policies, which could easily again become U.S. policies for a number of years.

Americans are undoubtedly divided on which presidency's policies were better for the country, but it is an uninformed or misinformed division. Most Americans never fully understood the choices Obama made in foreign policy nor the changes Trump made to that foreign policy.

As we see multiple conflicts exploding worldwide, along with U.S. involvement in wars and countering terrorism, Americans should be examining the choices made by Washington during the past twelve years in order to consider the best options for the immediate future. What were Obama's policies regarding ISIS, his methods to counter jihadists within the West, and his dealings with Russia and China? What informed these policies? Did they make Americans safer and more secure? Or was the Trump administration better at dealing with ISIS? Was he right to withdraw from the Iran deal? How has he handled countering jihadi penetration as well as Russia and China's challenges? And what, exactly, informed Trump's policies?

In my own view as a political scientist and a participant in international relations, but more importantly as someone who advised policy makers and opinion makers, I believe the Obama/Biden administration made multiple strategic mistakes which created several unresolved conflicts and national security challenges to be inherited by the Trump administration. I have also concluded that the Trump administration tried to reverse the course on a number of policies the previous administration had charted but was only partially successful in resolving such challenges and ending these threats. Two major reasons for that partial success, instead of full success: (1) the Obama mistakes were so serious and long term and (2) the bureaucracies operating under President Trump for the following four years were more inclined to apply Obama foreign policy—or at least resist the Trump changes.

Unfortunately, American media failed to provide accurate information to the public. This prevented them from understanding not only the differences between the policies of the two administrations—and their respective impacts on America's standing in the world—but also the direct national security interests of all Americans.

Broad Overview of Obama's Policies

One example of a complicit media can be seen in how the media in general praised the Iran deal, which was signed by the Obama administration, but never fully explained it to the American people, nor did a real debate take place before it became official.

As for the U.S. campaign against jihadi terrorism, the Obama-Biden administration did not designate the jihadi ideology as the root cause for that terrorism both in the Middle East and within the West. Last, but not least, the partnerships with extremist organizations such as the Muslim Brotherhood developed by the Obama administration were never given a justified rationale, and said partnerships eventually allowed a greater influence by these movements both in the region and at home.

Americans should be asking about the future of the Iran deal. They should want to know how the war against the jihadists will be won. They should be interested in how minorities and women and civil societies in the Middle East can be protected. They should understand what is important to American national security. They should understand if and when and how we support our allies overseas when they are facing threats. And Americans should understand how those threats across the globe impact their own national security.

If we do not address those threats in the Middle East and beyond, what price will we pay at home? Will the extremists around the world use the radicals at home to wreak havoc in America? Are the threats linked? Are we late in handling these menaces? What can and should be done now and in the next few years?

Of course, even from those who disagree with the decisions

made by Obama's administration, there are arguments against Trump that his administration was not fully successful in fulfilling his campaign promises—nor in fully changing the direction of Obama's foreign policy.

The real question, however, is: Which foreign policy is best for American national security at this point in time and at this juncture of history? The foreign policy of Obama and Biden? Or the foreign policy of Trump? These are two views starkly opposed to one another. And what will we be facing in 2021? We know that dangers are growing and accumulating, so it is crucial for Americans (and also for our allies) to make the right choices during the 2020 elections—and beyond.

CHAPTER 2

THE EMERGENCE OF OBAMA

There was a choice in 2008 as well.

During the 2008 primary campaigns, I endorsed former governor Mitt Romney based on his statements on national security and on the threats facing America—and on my knowledge of his thinking regarding future strategies the U.S. should adopt based on the recommendations of the 9/11 Commission of 2004 and the experiences of the Bush administration overseas and at home.

I already understood, thanks to the 2004 presidential elections, that Democrat candidate John Kerry would pull all U.S. forces away from the Middle East even before achieving the goals of establishing governments that would represent civil societies opposed to terrorism, which has been my vision since 2001— though, in reality, it was my vision even before that, during the 1990s. The platform adopted by John Kerry was a warning that his camp would, at the following round of elections in 2008, advocate the same views. I was concerned that the political opposition in the United States, namely the Democratic Party, had mutated from its left-of-center position, which had been embodied by politicians like the senator from Connecticut, Joe Lieberman, and other Democrat lawmakers who saw eye to eye with their fellow Republicans when it came to fighting the jihadi terrorists or containing the Iranian expansion.

That was the actual reason I chose Mitt Romney as the best possible candidate in 2008—even over John McCain, who was seen by many in the conservative camp as the tougher leader when it came to facing the terrorists (and who ultimately won the nomination of his party). But even in 2008, I knew that Romney understood that civil societies were the real long-term allies to the United States and the key coalition in the region for ensuring a sustained campaign in the war of ideas against the extremists. This was not a political component I saw in Senator McCain.

Romney lost in the primaries, so I supported Senator McCain despite the differences, simply because in the other camp there were no alternatives to the emerging two leaders. Hillary Clinton would have been an extension of former president Bill Clinton's eight years in the White House, which were representative of the complacency of the 1990s that was, in my view, responsible for the expansion of Iran and al-Qaeda, allowing and leading the way to the 9/11 attacks. However, from a sheer American national security perspective, the Clinton doctrines still presented a position of defense against terrorist activities.

Yet just as Romney lost the Republican nomination, Clinton did not win her party's nomination either. And with the new candidate, Barack Hussein Obama, the game completely changed inside the United States. The selection of a young state senator who became a U.S. senator in 2004 while calling on stopping actions in Iraq announced that an ideological shift had taken place in America. While the Clintons were the last expression of the left-of-center policies, the astonishing rise of Obama was an expression of a shift even further from that left of center—to the Far Left.

During the 2008 campaign, I was often on Arab media explaining the various ideas proposed by the candidates. I knew there was immense support for Barack Obama on behalf of the entire anti-American camp in the Middle East and their allies within the West, particularly among the supporters of the Muslim Brotherhood and of the Iranian regime. During one major debate at the BBC Arabic studios in Washington, D.C., U.S.-based supporters of the Far Left and the Brotherhood insisted that the victory of Obama was not only his victory but that it was signaling a deep shift in American politics that was going to change the mobilization that took place immediately after 9/11—they also argued that a backlash to counter-terrorism had produced a current of anti-intervention sympathetic to the Islamists.

Obama can be seen as the successful expression of millions of graduates from America's classrooms who had been indoctrinated by Far Left and Islamist apologists. As I argued in my book the year before, in 2007, titled *The War of Ideas*, the American classroom indeed was sending its graduates to the newsroom, the courtroom, and the war room, thus creating an organized wave of support for the left-wing alternative to the Bush doctrine, whose policies centered on fighting terrorism and countering the extremist agenda of the Islamists and of Iran.

In my view, the only candidate who would have been able to at least intellectually challenge the Obama platform was (ironically) Mitt Romney, but with his loss in the primaries to Senator McCain, the Obama agenda was easily crushing Republican talking points because McCain represented the Republicans of the Cold War who were still fighting the Soviet Union and had no problem allying with the "mujahideen"— a mistake made decades earlier that even Bush had managed to avoid during his seven years fighting the jihadists.

Barack Obama entered national politics with a fully formed platform created in the labs of America's academia. Once elected, the world would quickly learn who the young intellectual president known to be a community organizer really was.

I gave a warning to many members of Congress and in several interviews on Fox News in 2008 and early 2009: The incoming administration was not simply a new Democrat in the White House. No, America was going to be experiencing a new political doctrine—one that had never before been tested in U.S. politics, not even during the Carter presidency. Obama was bringing with him two forces. The first was a new ideological agenda centered on the principle that America had done wrong in the past under both Republicans and Democrats in the White House and that the country should change course not just in terms of domestic policies but also massively shift regarding foreign policy and national security.

Obama aimed at repositioning the United States, moving from being clearly on the side of the anti-jihadist camp and pro-freedom bloc to somewhere in between—with the eventual goal of pushing the country to partner with extreme ideological factions in the Arab and Muslim world. He also sought a change of policy regarding Russia, China, and the Marxist forces in Latin America.

I clearly saw the links between the Obama team and the world of radicals and apologists to extremist regimes and movements in the Greater Middle East and beyond while touring campuses and think tanks throughout the nineties and in the early years after 9/11. Barack Obama was the best possible candidate for such a movement to succeed in general elections. In the Democratic primaries, the public could not clearly see the strategic differences between Hillary Clinton and the young senator from Illinois. Hillary Clinton was a social Democrat, left of center, while Obama sat solidly on the Far Left of the traditional establishment of the Democratic Party. Most Americans probably did not see the more important difference, however: the arrival on the national scene of an elite produced on campuses during the previous decade and a half.

What worried me as the Obama administration took over in January of 2009 was the idea that the full power of the most formidable democracy on the planet was going to fall into the hands of a new establishment that aligned very closely to the radical regimes and movements in the Middle East and Africa as well as in Latin America. Those worries turned out to be justified. But the other concern I had at the time was how America could ever re-emerge from such a transformational shift. The sacrifices it would take to bring the United States back on course would be monumental. The cost to bridge the gap created by four or eight years of such an administration would be immense.

The architects of the Obama administration were very smart as they played the card of a candidate who could, just by being elected, resolve an acute domestic wound that had been oozing since the Civil War and had never been fully resolved, even after the early 1960s. His election could finally celebrate racial equality should an African American become the president of the United States. Ideally, this would have happened in America in the late sixties with Dr. Martin Luther King. Unfortunately, history decided otherwise, and it took multiple presidencies to find the opportunity for that historical justice to be served.

The problem was that justice was served with the right symbol but the wrong African American politician, especially when it came to foreign policy. President Obama did not side with the oppressed societies overseas in general nor in the Middle East in particular. In fact, he sided with oppressive regimes like the

Iranian regime—and radical organizations like the Muslim Brotherhood. Ideally, an African American leader would have brought social justice inside America and at the same time stood firmly with ethnic minorities in foreign policy, starting at least with East Africa, where the population of Darfur and South Sudan as well as Bejas and Berbers were looking forward to the ascension of an American president with African roots to get the attention of the American people after decades of abandonment. One would also hope that consistent policy of supporting the oppressed would have also meant hope for the Yazidi and Christian minorities in the Levant.

President Barack Hussein Obama had an admirable speech style, excelled at gestures and symbolism, and successfully connected with the youth, but when it came to substance of policies, his administration sided with authoritarian radicals instead of civil societies overseas. The problem was his political strategic agenda.

CHAPTER 3

A RADICAL SHIFT

Soon after landing in the White House, President Obama initiated two major moves, which by the end of May or early June 2009 indicated where his administration was going in terms of national security and foreign policy. It was obvious to me at the time that the country was veering away from the post-9/11 posture and the so-called War on Terror and heading in the opposite direction of demobilization of America on the one hand and the activation of an apologist policy on the other in order to engage with future partners who were actually at the core of terrorism and extremism.

Most Americans in the early years of the Obama administration focused on the domestic agenda and therefore did not see or understand the much wider change of direction that the new team at the White House was implementing: the eventual dismantling of the War on Terror and with it the war of ideas. In other words, the Obama doctrine was telling Americans that our conflict with the radicals overseas was in error because the conflict was caused by us—and therefore we need not only to cease our efforts of resistance against the jihadists, Iran, and the other radicals but jump on a train going in the other direction, one that would lead us to engaging the foes and finding agreement with each of them in order to transform American policy overseas.

The first major benchmark that indicated a massive Obama-Biden change in foreign policy with implications on national security was Obama's trip to Egypt in spring 2009 and his address at Cairo University. The main idea of President Obama on the political philosophy level was to inform the American public that the United States has been seen as an aggressor against Arabs and Muslims since 9/11—maybe even decades before that. This perception prevailed on U.S. campuses for decades among leftist academics and intellectuals. It was explained as the American branch of Western colonialism. But the urgency behind this U-turn made by the administration in foreign policy perception was in fact linked to how the United States reacted to the 9/11 attacks.

In my own experiences after the 2001 jihadist strikes against New York, D.C., and elsewhere, the immediate reaction after al-Qaeda suicide missions on American soil was explained by a combination of Far Left and neo-Marxist circles actually accusing the United States of *provoking* the attacks. During the seven years of the Bush administration, both the Islamist lobbies and their Red allies in America were organizing to oppose any form of American self-defense and thus did oppose both the war in

Afghanistan and the one in Iraq while also framing them as neocolonialist conquests.

It was imperative for the Obama team to change the national security doctrine that had been approved by a unanimous and bipartisan 9/11 Commission to align with their own narrative. The reality was that for years, before the Obama victory in 2008, a new alliance was being forged between the Islamists in general (the Muslim Brotherhood and the Khomeinist Iranians in particular) and the core left-wing neo-Marxists within the West in general (and the United States in particular). The Obama group belonged to that core—a subset found mostly on campuses but also in parts of the media.

With the alliance already in place, it made sense for the new administration to unleash its plans as early as possible. Hence, Obama's 2009 address in Cairo was essentially an open invitation through public acknowledgment of his desire for a partnership between his administration and the Muslim Brotherhood. Though Egypt was ruled by authoritarian President Mubarak, Obama's visit and his praise of the Ikhwan talking points were the opening salvo of a campaign designed to crumble the Egyptian regime and, later, other Arab governments—and replace them with the Brotherhood. The genesis of the Islamization of the Arab Spring of 2011 thus started in 2009.

The Obama speech at Cairo University, in fact, officialized a partnership between the United States and the Muslim Brotherhood, and in general terms with the Islamist movements in the MENA region. One might think that such a move would be checked by the mainstream Republican Party in D.C., but it was not—due to the equal impact of the Qatar and Islamist lobbies on the Republican institution. It did, however, unnerve the conservative sectors of the Republicans both in Congress and in the grassroots while also putting pressure on the traditional liberals in the Democratic Party after the ilk of Joe Lieberman and others.

The major shift towards engaging the Islamists worldwide also opened the door for partnerships with their lobbies and NGOs inside the United States. This led to an unstoppable rise of influence of militant groups such as CAIR (Council on American-Islamic Relations), which in turn became the spearhead of a campaign to silence the critics against Obama's new policies in Congress and in the media.

But a shift to align with the Muslim Brotherhood was not the only onslaught of the Obama administration in foreign policy; it was simply the first one. Indeed, in the same month of June 2009, President Obama engaged in a second track that would change another U.S. national security policy, one that was established in the early 1980s: the containment of the Islamic Republic of Iran.

In early June 2009, President Barack Obama addressed a letter to the Grand Ayatollah of Iran, Imam Ali Khamenei, calling on him to begin a new era of cooperation between Tehran and Washington. That letter, which was as apologist as the speech to the Muslim Brotherhood weeks earlier in Cairo, signaled the beginning of a long process that would lead to the negotiation and signing of the Iran nuclear deal in 2015. But June 2009 had one more surprise that revealed a third shocking policy shift, one that would divert the country from its longstanding tradition of helping nations facing oppression and seeking freedom.

Indeed, America, in one century—between the First World War, the Second World War, and the collapse of the Soviet Union—had demonstrated its commitment, through blood and treasure, to stand by peoples on many continents as they had been brutalized and oppressed—from Europe and the Middle East to Asia and Latin America. But the events in Iran at the end of June 2009 signaled a drastic third policy change. Millions of Iranians, including many women, took to the streets to protest the suppression by the regime. Many of these protesters held signs in English—one of which called on President Obama by name to help them. Yet to reaffirm that the U.S. would not "meddle" in Iranian politics or stand with the democratic revolution in Iran, a second letter was sent to Khamenei on September 3.

The abandonment by the Obama administration of the Green Revolution in Iran was the benchmark that told me that the American policy of supporting freedom fighters and people's uprisings against totalitarian governments, the praise for dissidents, and the backing of free societies around the world had ended.

2009 was the year that broke the backbone of post-Cold War U.S. foreign policy and rebuilt it into a radical approach inconsistent with the feelings and perceptions of the majority of Americans. Yet most Americans were not informed and educated enough, particularly by their academia and media, to correct such radicalization of policy via their members of Congress—or to elect a new president who would change directions one more time to align policy to once again be consistent with U.S. national security and traditional American liberty principles.

Fears for the Future

Both the Cedar Revolution in Lebanon in 2005 and the Green Revolution in Iran in 2009 provided indications that peoples in the region had reached critical mass in regard to their tolerance for authoritarians and would eventually protest and demand change. Social media has also evolved and has become much more accessible by ordinary people. In my book *The Coming Revolution*, I predicted that most countries in the Arab world were going to witness social and political unrests, results I had been waiting for, for many years, to push back against the extremists.

I briefed many members of Congress during that same period of time and convinced them that there were authentic forces of change in the region, including seculars, women, and minorities, and that the United States should immediately partner with them as the authoritarian leaders were going down—and fighting a lost battle to support ailing dictators would not be the right battle for the United States.

My concern was that the moment would be squandered as the Obama administration was racing to connect with the Islamists and the Iranians in the region and thus diverting the resources of the U.S. government to the wrong factions instead of helping civil society forces. I observed how the lobbies of our traditional foes were moving with great speed at all levels within the bureaucracies and the administration. I was also receiving many complaints from Middle East human rights and minorities groups that officials and governments were no longer engaging them like the Bush administration had tried to do. In addition, members of Congress in the Republican opposition (who won the majority in the U.S. House of Representatives in 2010) were sharing their fears that the administration had abandoned our allies in the region, not just allies among Middle East minorities, but also Israel. So by the end of 2009, early 2010, I could see the whole picture, and it was a dark and dire one.

CHAPTER 4

THE ARAB SPRING DRAMA

When the protests began in early 2011, the Republican and conservative side in Washington was very skeptical of engaging with "rebels" and preferred to stay with leaders they knew, such as Mubarak of Egypt, Gaddafi of Libya, Ali Abdullah Saleh of Yemen, and even Assad of Syria. They were afraid of the unknown and of "screaming people" on the streets, even though we were encouraging them to identify the right moderate and secular forces. Unfortunately, the Obama-Biden administration had by then successfully reversed the network of engagement with such dissidents and the democratic forces the Bush administration had reached out to and partially revived.

There were some Republicans willing to return to the Bush platform of supporting the freedom fighters, even actively, but the more conservative side of the Republican party wanted to stick with the authoritarians with whom the U.S. had traditionally done business.

But I knew that between 2009 and 2011, the Obama administration had already connected to networks of Islamist armies across North Africa and the Middle East and the bureaucracies were already engaged with the Muslim Brotherhood on the one hand and the pro-Iranian movements on the other to try to replace the ailing dictators with Islamist-led governments. Obama was prepared and committed to intervening in the Arab Spring while the conservatives in Washington had no plans whatsoever to deal with the matter.

Since 2001 and throughout my years in D.C., including six years with the Foundation for Defense of Democracies (FDD), I had assembled an impressive web of contacts with NGOs and human rights organizations across the MENA region and was constantly updated about the feelings, aspirations, and plans of civil society forces from Indonesia to Iran. Starting in January 2011, I received several panicky messages from the region and from communities in the homeland that the Obama administration had already partnered with what they called the "wrong guys" in the region and that the revolutions were being lost. I was urged to reach out to the Obama administration to correct the steps. Unfortunately, the executive branch had already made up its mind and was not responsive to the various outreaches I organized from the House of Representatives with the help of Republican and at times even Democratic members.

Middle Eastern and liberal Muslim groups petitioned the

State Department and the White House several times during that Arab Spring via the offices of members of Congress, but alas with no reaction from the White House. The dice had already been thrown, and in my view, disaster was inevitable.

What made the position of the Republican camp difficult to unify was the fact that it had one wing who ignored the dissidents and stuck with the dictators, a large center that wanted to continue the Bush-type outreach to freedom forces, and (unfortunately) another wing that was still influenced by the Cold War and had not absorbed the changes that took place in 2001. That most problematic wing was led by Senator John McCain's circle and believed that the "rebels" who were Islamists were actually the *right* partners to ally with. Hence, the wide coalition in Washington that endorsed the Brotherhood and their allies in the region was comprised of the Obama administration and Democrats—and the Republican wing influenced by the Islamists. Senator McCain was a fighter against the Soviet threat, no doubt about it. He also was good at countering Iran's menace. Up until 2008, he opposed what he called "radical Islam." But since he lost to Obama and particularly since the start of the Arab Spring, something changed. He became sympathetic to Qatar and the Muslim Brotherhood. Other politicians moved in the same direction.

With help from individual members of Congress and members of the European Parliament, as well as NGOs, we tried our best to have the Atlantic alliance seize an historic opportunity in the Arab Spring to side with the right partners, those who support democracy and pluralism and who expressed a commitment to protect minorities. Our goal was to empower these segments to ensure that the radicals did not seize power and build Islamist regimes.

The Western alliance had removed one marginal form of fundamentalist power in Afghanistan, the Taliban, in the reaction to 9/11. My fear was that the Obama administration was going to replace the single Taliban regime taken out by the Bush administration and replace it with five or six other similar regimes in the region, ruled by the Muslim Brotherhood and their jihadi associates. Unfortunately, those crucial first twelve months of the Arab Spring took place too early for the possibility of an alternative policy to come out of Washington via a new administration. The presidential elections were in November of 2012. Even if a Romney administration had been formed, it would not have taken over until the end of January 2013. By then, the Obama administration would have already empowered the Brotherhood across the region...because that is exactly what happened.

Three Revolutions of the Arab Spring

LIBYA

In Libya, Gaddafi was resisting the revolt while the Obama administration and the Sarkozy government of France led a NATO mission to crumble his regime. I definitely was no fan of

Muammar Gaddafi, whom I had been criticizing since the eighties in my motherland, but as the Atlantic alliance was pounding his forces, I was voicing concerns about who would replace him. My analysis of the input I was obtaining from footage on Al Jazeera and from my conversations with Libyan diplomats, including the Libya ambassador to Washington, was drawing a negative image.

The "rebels" were a collection of three components:

1. the liberals who had the louder expression in European and American media,

2. the actual military and bureaucratic dissidents of the Gaddafi regime, and

3. the most dangerous—the jihadists and their Islamist allies.

It appeared that the most dangerous component had the most organized lobby in Washington and was actually coordinating with the Obama administration and those Republican members of the Senate who were in full support of the Islamist component of the revolution, whom they called "rebels."

I had established, along with conservative U.S. and European lawmakers, some contacts with liberal Libyan NGOs and held conferences in D.C., Madrid, and Brussels to examine the means by which to navigate the Western response to the Arab upheavals. I agreed with the former prime minister of Spain, who had influence on the majority-EPP party in the European Parliament, that the faster we could find moderate elements from the region and engage with them, the better the outcome would be. One of the first meetings was held in Madrid at the FAES institute. But events on the ground in Libya and the rest of North Africa and the Levant were moving much faster than we were.

A number of former diplomats, bureaucrats, and military personnel of the Libyan government were trying to reach out to Europeans and Americans. In Libya, for example, Chief of Staff General Yunis was organizing the rebel military and planning on protecting the moderate and secular activists on the one hand and reaching out to NATO on the other hand. This option would have been the best one available and would have opened the path for a civilian government with an option to transition to a democracy. But apparently, the Muslim Brotherhood militias assassinated the general, seized the weapons in depots, marginalized the seculars, and announced themselves as the only viable rebels in Libya.

Immediately, the Obama administration and the McCain group in the Senate hooked up with the Muslim Brotherhood and recognized them as the official partner of Washington. A victorious revolution and Libya ended up with a transitional regime dominated by the Brotherhood, and the American public did not understand a single thing about what was happening. We lost Libya to the bad guys thanks to the Obama partnership with the Ikhwan.

TUNISIA AND YEMEN

The very same dilemma took place as U.S. policy was addressing the revolutions in Tunisia, Yemen, and Syria. And the same model of partnering with the Islamist movements instead of secular democrats was applied. The Obama-Biden administration was fulfilling the implied promises of the Cairo speech.

The administration had a preexisting relationship between the Tunisia-based Islamist Nahda Party led by Ghannouchi, who was in exile, and he was swiftly assisted to seize power in Tunis after the fall of President Ben Ali. And just as in Egypt, Washington was split in three:

1. The traditional Republicans from the Bush era and those who were core conservatives sided with President Ben Ali and expressed frustration because of the speed with which President Obama pressured the authoritarian leader to resign and go into exile in Saudi Arabia.

2. Cold War-era Republicans who saw an ally in the Islamists.

3. A middle way option adopted by a few members of Congress and Tunisian Americans who wanted to find connections with the first wave of the revolution—which was clearly civil society, made up of workers, women, and students.

Obviously, I supported the third group—and at the early stage of the revolution in Tunisia, as an author of the only book that predicted the Arab Spring, *The Coming Revolution* of 2010, I was all over the media again explaining that the first leap by most of these societies in the MENA region was clearly one of moderate members of civil societies.

In Yemen, a pro-Iranian insurgency by those known as the Houthis took place within the Shia community in the north. Incidents from the Houthis against Saudi security and Yemeni governments had been taking place since 2009, strangely, since the Obama administration was formed. In 2011 and in the wake of the revolutions of Tunisia, Egypt, and Syria, civil society across Yemen erupted against the government of Ali Abdullah Saleh. Again, a comparable scenario took place in Washington where the administration called on Saleh to resign, announced its support to the revolution, and called on the armed forces not to intervene.

But the reality was that the Obama administration favored the elements in the north close to the pro-Iranian Houthis and elements from the Islah Party closer to the Muslim Brotherhood. Ironically, the Southern progressive movement, which was in the past closer to Marxist left-wing ideology, was ignored by the progressive allies of the Obama administration. Liberals and leftist factions in Yemen found themselves isolated while the pro-Iran and pro-Ikhwan factions gave their own NGOs and political parties the label of rebels and used this description to win support within the United States and (partially) in Western Europe.

These Islamist forces, in Libya, Tunisia, Egypt, and both North and South Yemen, usurped the diplomatic and moral support from the U.S. from the original civil society forces. At the time I also understood that the administration's policy toward

Saudi Arabia was to again favor the two major partners announced in June of 2009, the Muslim Brotherhood and the supporters of Iran, in preparation for what would become the Iran deal few years later.

SYRIA

The drama in Syria was more complicated and very intense. By March 2011, demonstrations by civil society groups, students, workers, and democracy groups spread from Damascus to other cities and towns across the country, calling for reforms and eventually for the resignation of Bashar Assad.

In the first few months of the uprising against the Syrian dictator, the U.S. ambassador to Damascus took the side of the demonstrators, which in my view meant that Washington wanted Assad to make concessions and eventually accept the formation of a reformist government. The previous year, Secretary of State Hillary Clinton had called Bashar Assad a "reformer." That situation in Syria presented a major challenge to the Obama administration because on the one hand, Assad was the ally of the Iranian regime and the White House was feverishly working on engaging the Iranians. On the other hand, the White House had been working with Muslim Brotherhood teams since 2009 to prepare for alternatives to various Arab regimes in Sunni-majority countries. Syria presented a challenge because the regime was Alawi, a branch of Shia (and the Brotherhood groups operated in *Sunni*-majority countries).

Those who started the revolt against Assad were liberal and were composed of moderate elements of society. There was a clear shot for the non-Islamist and anti-Assad popular uprising to win the battle and force Assad to accept change without compromising Syria to the Islamists. That was my view, the view of a number of members of Congress, the view of the human rights community, and even of some elements at the State Department who opposed Assad on the grounds of the violence he had practiced on the opposition. I pushed for the withdrawal of Assad's forces, at least towards his own Alawi areas in the northwest of Syria to allow for the formation of an interim government which would represent all communities of Syria, including the Sunnis, to form the new constitutional structures of the Syrian Republic. I had envisaged, after speaking with many minorities representatives in the country, that a federal system could be adopted in Syria, giving autonomy to Kurds, Christians, and Druze, and allowing full democracy within the Sunni-majority areas. But time was of essence.

Various jihadi groups were organizing and penetrating the region, and the regime was using mass violence against the demonstrators, eventually clashing with the moderate armed elements. Within a few months, the middle-ground moderate protesters were being crushed between the regime on one hand and the jihadists on the other.

The hesitation of the Obama administration was due to his own dilemma. He struggled with satisfying the lobbying of the

Muslim Brotherhood, who were pushing for a backing to the Islamist militias (in reality, jihadi groups) while under the pressure of pro-Iran lobbies to not push hard on Assad because Assad's collapse would mean a collapse of negotiations with Iran. What added to the problem was that the Qatar Ikhwan lobbying efforts in Washington influenced a small segment of former Cold War warriors in the Republican party, including the McCain group in the U.S. Senate, who strongly lobbied to support what they called "rebels" against Assad while indirectly and maybe inadvertently backing the Islamic militias.

The Ikhwan and Iran lobbies vying over U.S. policy regarding Syria were stronger than any campaign pro-human rights and minorities groups have ever been able to develop in Washington, D.C. I did what I could at the time to explain to Congress and in the media the choice made in Syria should be to partner with moderate Sunnis and all other minorities, including Kurds.

To no avail. The administration finally chose to accept a balance between the Assad and Brotherhood lobbies, dropping the minorities and the Sunni moderates. The damage from the failure to once again back moderate dissidents was immediately felt, and the window that allowed Sunni moderates to demonstrate was closed, and the marches were crushed by early 2012. The major players in Syria were the regime and its Hezbollah and Iran allies plus a militarized opposition that was slowly but surely seized by either jihadists or by Islamist militias backed by the AKP government of Turkey. As the presidential campaign ramped up in early 2012, the Obama White House had already lost Syria to the competition between radical groups within the country.

Arab Spring Crushed

The baby steps of the Arab Spring were crushed by the radicals from all sides. The administration, through its strategic choices, killed the possible birth of a civil society revolution in the Arab world. Obviously, those upheavals would not have translated into liberal democracies overnight, but had it not been for U.S. support to the Islamist movements across the region and the unwillingness by the White House to confront Iran's allies in the Arab world, some form of Arab Spring could have succeeded. Had American foreign policy instead focused on democracy groups and secular democrats in the MENA region, this would have at least given hope to the peoples of the Middle East and supported their movement in the right direction.

Unfortunately, the Obama-Biden administration, because of its partnership with the two worst forces in the region, either willfully or inadvertently unleashed the forces of extremism for another decade. There was only one option possible to try to change the directions of events in the region: taking the case to the American public. Thus, as the November 2012 presidential election was fast approaching, it was important to support an alternative platform to the Obama administration, and the only option available by 2011 was a Republican candidate able to challenge the administration with a different agenda in hopes that the American voters would change the direction in foreign policy—especially regarding the Greater Middle East.

CHAPTER 5

THE 2012 ELECTION:
OBAMA VS. ROMNEY

Back in 2008, I had already determined that compared to the other Republican candidates, including Senator John McCain, Mitt Romney seemed to be the most sophisticated in his statements, especially in the way he framed the threats of jihadism and the Iranian regime. McCain was right on target regarding the Iranian threat, Assad and Hezbollah, but was off target on the Islamists. Romney understood the strategic dimension of what I envisaged as a war of ideas. He was in full agreement with the idea of finding allies in the Middle East, first among civil societies, but also putting together a coalition of countries willing to engage in counterterrorism with the United States.

As the Obama administration was transforming U.S. foreign policy into a monster I disagreed with, and after I saw the White House developing a partnership with the Islamists and approaching the Ayatollahs, I felt that a second Romney campaign was the only viable and institutional way to stop the downward slide; for it took just a few years to realize that all the gains made in awareness and strategic preparedness under the Bush administration were gone. The way many lawmakers and I saw it, four more years of Obama foreign policy would be to the detriment of American national security and possibly make it irretrievable.

The change of majority in the House of Representatives in 2010 was a signal that many Americans disagreed with the White House agenda both in domestic and foreign policies. Practically, however, the flipping of the House majority from support to the administration to the opposition did not yield significant change in foreign affairs. The influence of the two lobbies continued to grow, Russia was shifting from less interested in the region to more interested in engaging Iran, and the latter's control of the Middle East was solidifying. A 2012 victory for a Romney presidency would help, but without adjusting the foreign policy that was allowing our geopolitical foes to gain ground overseas and without limiting the lobbies' expansion within the bureaucracies, it would be very difficult to reverse the damage without paying a very high price.

When I joined the Romney campaign, I worked with a number of senior advisers, many of whom came from the Bush administration, some even from the Bush (41) and Reagan teams. Some of them, including Robert O'Brien, later served with the

Trump Administration. Though the candidate (and others) were in line with the Bush and 9/11 Commission guidelines, many among the higher-ups in the campaign still had a Cold War mindset and very few had absorbed and understood the post-9/11 realities. In addition, while we shared some strategies with the neocons, it was evident they were not ready for a transformative foreign policy. They maintained a status quo that was not winning the War on Terror in Afghanistan, nor in Iraq, and certainly not at the level of the war of ideas. While many in the base wanted to see a strong response being developed to stop the Obama agenda, a response more intelligent and sophisticated than the Republican campaign's response in 2008, I realized some of the barons of the Cold War were also those close to the idea of conducting business with Iran, as well as staying close to what they believed were conservative Muslims, who in reality were the Muslim Brotherhood. Those barons kept Romney chained to the heavy inertia that brought down the Bush platform against terrorism and grinded any positive movement to a standstill.

Because of my experience in international relations and my vast network of contacts in many countries, including in Europe and in the Middle East, I developed multiple tracks on which to engage with politicians, members of governments, lawmakers, and think tanks around the world to discuss their views and the candidate's views in preparation for what could become a Romney administration.

I have to admit, though, that the Obama campaign backed by

his bureaucracy and the Democratic body had a much wider, stronger, and better-funded web of international relations, with dozens of advisers, experts, and specialists roaming the world in support of Obama's international image. Back in the 2008 campaign, Obama's activities overseas were to promote his image at home of an experienced leader, hence his speech in Berlin and his visit to Israel. But in 2012, Obama had already scored many points, starting with a Nobel Peace Prize and multiple summits, visits, opportunities, and speeches. He did not need more recognition to convince voters that he could assume an office with world responsibilities, but his campaign was nevertheless engaged worldwide, unlike the Republican campaigns of 2008 and 2012, which had limited abilities, fewer contacts, and above all, had not yet set up a sophisticated platform.

Romney had his own vision, which he outlined in his book and in some of his speeches, but many of his aides put a priority on getting to the White House first and developing the policies later. And the impetus behind this reasoning was that the machinery of the party and of the previous Republican administration under George Bush was ready to move, yet they had no interest in a new Romney doctrine. They wanted to prolong either the Bush policies and commitments or even some Cold War views.

Meanwhile, I advised engaging with the majority-conservative party in Europe, the EPP, or the Christian democrats in order to learn from their experiences. I also advised engaging with representatives from civil societies across the MENA region in addition to having discussions with leaders from Latin America and East Asia. In early October 2012, I attended the European policy conference in Berlin and received many questions about Romney's international policies. My speech centered on the need to push back against indoctrination and radicalization produced by the Muslim Brotherhood, warning that a new more lethal jihadi terror group could emerge in Syria and Iraq if the moderates are abandoned. I also called for putting pressure on the Iranian regime to pull back its militias from Iraq, Syria, and Lebanon.

The last effort I undertook in defense of Romney's foreign policy and national security of the homeland was to launch a large coalition of Arab-Muslim and Middle Eastern Americans across the country who supported the agenda of the Republican campaign under Romney. The American Middle East Coalition (AMC) for Romney included Iranians, Lebanese, Syrians, Iraqis, Egyptians, Sudanese, some members of Kurdish community, Assyrians, Chaldeans, Syriac Copts, Yazidis, and other minorities. It also represented Catholics, Maronites, Protestants, and all factions originating in the region. This was in response to the charges from the Obama camp that only he could attract votes from Muslims and Arabs. The launch of the AMC proved that Americans from Middle Eastern descent could support not only a Republican platform (and many did even before the launch of the coalition) on socio-economic grounds but also on the grounds of foreign policy; for we made the case that a Romney administration would support civil societies and the region's religious freedom, minority rights, and moderate majorities. This again was another challenge, not just for the Obama camp but also for the radical circles overseas who were concerned that a defeat of the Obama presidency would put an end to the growth of their influence in Washington, D.C.

I felt that the foreign affairs portfolio of the campaign was solid enough to sail through the elections and a transition and eventually take grip inside the new administration. However, my experiences during the campaign and my perception of the other foreign policy circles around the campaign convinced me that even if Mitt Romney was elected president of the United States there would definitely be a struggle within his own administration to affirm the direction of foreign policy because the remnants of the Bush administration were not all on the same page with regard to the future. The only hope was that the candidate himself knew the subject enough to be able to survive the advising body, and that was crucial for me in any future choice.

But Romney lost. At the level of national mobilization, it was obvious the media machine of the Obama camp was much larger and much more assertive. Romney's political machine could not compete. The Cold War barons of the Republican campaign were dealing with a new type of fighting machine in Obama, one they were unprepared to go to battle with. The former community organizer brought the Marxist militant type of movement to American politics, a process which in the past had always taken place between considerate and measured parties. The Obama machine was more of a European popular mass organization backed by a ferocious media arm which knew no mercy and held no ethics. The real victory of militant Obama in 2012 against the gentleman Romney was actually achieved in 2008 against the classical McCain. American politics changed after Bush. There was an infusion of some "third-world-ism" into the already contentious American party politics.

Why This Is Important Now

Experts in U.S. presidential politics may weigh in with other ideas, but it seemed to me in 2012 that the Republican machine backing Romney was inherited from the Bush campaign—which had spent four years outside the circles of power and disconnected from the mass transformations on campuses. The Romney campaign missed many opportunities, one of which was open for grabs. The party missed significant opportunities to connect with Hispanics. I, personally, through the Middle East Coalition, connected with many Latino groups seeking mobilization under the campaign. At one of the debates in 2012, one of the leaders asked the candidates if there was any special message to Hispanic conservatives. The answer by Newt Gingrich at the time was that there is no special answer for special ethnic groups: "We are all Americans," he said. While the goal was definitely for all ethnic groups to merge into one American national identity, it was still a fact that the country was made of various ethnic groups seeking to merge. The Republican campaign needed to show these ethnic communities (Latin American, African American, Middle Eastern

American, and Asian American, to name a few) how they contribute to a single national identity with multiple ethnic roots, the actual story of America. The Democratic platform had excessive statements on ethnic minorities, which they called "race," but the reality was that the Democrats wanted to maintain the ethnic and so-called "race card" as long as possible as a political tool while the Republican platform *should* have recognized unique contributions while encouraging all communities to move in a united direction formulated from all diversity of input.

The great battle of 2012 was not only an American one. Many forces worldwide, including regimes and international networks, took part in the pressures to convince American voters to choose Obama over Romney. The idea behind international media's involvement was to demonstrate that foreign media would show an American public that the world is shifting towards one of the two candidates. Such a move is, in fact, meddling, but such "meddling" is open and free as long as it does not interfere with the voting process. International media and social media played a role in the 2012 elections that was more a psychological component than a direct interference. And here again the Obama machine was by far more experienced and adept at shifting international perceptions.

The dynamics in 2016 had to take on the same impossible stakes. The same massive and integrated political machine, backed by an incumbent presidency, bureaucracy, and media.

Only another outsider, only another shift in thinking and tactics, would be able to compete in this new political era. Only a fearless, charismatic persona could go up against the militant political machine created by Obama. Only a candidate without compunction or hesitation could face such a merciless and powerful adversary.

Meanwhile...

While the 2012 campaign was progressing on the home front, major events were taking place overseas, including in the Greater Middle East. In Egypt, the Muslim Brotherhood movement had secured the control of government, managing to get its leader Mohamed Morsi elected as a president. Evidence indicates that the pro-Ikhwan NGOs backed by Washington played a role in shaping victory toward Morsi. Half of his voters were non-Islamists who believed that his candidacy was to consolidate the first uprising against authoritarian Mubarak. Apparently, the army was pressured by the Pentagon to sideline themselves and not speak up against the Islamists. In short, the Obama administration was efficient in sweeping the fundamentalists into power in the midst of U.S. presidential elections.

In Libya, a similar scenario (though more violent) was taking place. In the wake of the killing of Gaddafi, U.S. support was granted to Brotherhood-backed groups, which practically seized power in Tripoli. That same year, al-Nahda was also backed morally and politically by the Obama-Biden team and further empowered into the political institutions. Similar positions were taken regarding the Islamist factions in Syria and Yemen. By the time the terror attack took place against the U.S. consulate in Benghazi in September 2012, the campaign had reached its peak with the Romney versus Obama debates. Unfortunately, in my view, Romney lost opportunities to expose Obama's foreign policies in the midst of the Arab Spring and missed strategic moments to criticize the both the administration's partnership with the Islamists and the Iran policy of the White House, a failure his political advisors are to be blamed for. This may have even contributed to less warmth from the Christian and conservative communities who were observing these events in MENA.

With the failure of the Romney campaign, President Obama and VP Biden gained four more years to solidify and expand their foreign policy. This second term saw the implementation of grand designs from the Obama White House both overseas and at home. In my view, these were the most perilous four years in modern American history since the Cuban Missile Crisis. In fact, some of the policies implemented were even more dangerous than those at the peak of the Cold War. Even during the confrontation with the Soviet Union, it was less likely that Moscow would unilaterally engage in a nuclear war, but Obama's engagement in the nuclear deal with Iran was empowering a regime that had no ideological restraint from using these ultimate apocalyptic weapons once conditions were met.

I have been arguing since 9/11 that with the Communists

being atheist, they had to calculate very meticulously that should they engage in a nuclear war, not only did they need to win it decisively and quickly, but they also had to make sure that their populations and their leadership would be safe—because the Soviets had no ideological doctrines that ensured an afterlife for which they could sacrifice lives here and now. In contrast, the Khomeinist regime of Tehran is all about fundamentalism where death is not a deterrent, and in fact their promotion of suicide bombing as a weapon is an indication of a militaristic theology, which does not account for civilian casualties because in their doctrine, activities they are engaged in while alive serve as an interim or preparation for the afterlife—or paradise.

CHAPTER 6

OBAMA & BIDEN STRATEGIES IN THE MIDDLE EAST

The desired achievements of the White House after the 2012 election were an Iran deal and a partnership with the Muslim Brotherhood.

What few understood in 2012 was the much larger agenda the Obama team had behind the idea of a partnership with the Islamists across the region. Beyond the strategy of becoming allies to what were described as "moderate Islamists" lay another invisible goal. Middle Eastern studies academia in America, and prior to that in Britain, argued, with some neo-Marxist notions, that the middle class-led Muslim Brotherhood was erecting a caliphate that could somehow become "progressive." Obviously, the academic work standing behind this White House doctrine comprehended neither the history of the region nor in general terms how social forces within   large socio-religious blocs operated.

There were even a few times President Obama mentioned Islam like post-Soviet Marxists would: as a "powerful organizational force." Rare were those in Washington who understood what the former community organizer really meant. Obama looked at Islam not just as a religion but as a vast network of committed people who could be a force used to obstruct some policies and give strength to other policies.

It did not make sense that a neo-Marxist would believe in the "theological" goal of a caliphate. The only realistic explanation was that the neo-Marxists of the twenty-first century wanted to use the Islamists as a tool to achieve the goal of a *geopolitical* caliphate, a regime that would provide control over peoples' lands and, most importantly, resources, that they would then have access to—and maybe even power over. Extrapolating this to the realities surrounding the partnership with the Islamists, by backing them to seize power in several countries, this would create a regional power that would reflect their ideology and the elite in power would offer to participate in the accumulated wealth. In this case, the wealth could be oil, gas, and energy to be extracted and sold. In exceptional cases, it could mean the cash of a crumbling country like Libya.

The U.S. Constitution and American foreign policy cannot accommodate such a raw vision without clashing with the American public and international community. An administration cannot openly support radical groups or regimes to take over a region and then claim control of its resources in the interests of the U.S. government. And perhaps that is why most Americans cannot understand the strategic thinking behind such foreign policy. But if one were to consider not the financial interests of the U.S. government but private financial interests linked to international financial interests, a different strategic reading of the Obama policies between 2009 and 2016 in the Greater Middle East can be summarized as both empowering the Muslim Brotherhood to seize power from the Atlantic to Gaza and cutting a deal with the Ayatollahs allowing them to seize power from Tehran to Beirut. Obviously, such a grand and global vision can only be achieved through formal agreements with both blocs.

That is what is at stake. If Americans do not think this is what was behind Obama's foreign policy, perhaps the evidence will sway them otherwise.

Egypt

The administration's policy on Egypt after 2009 was to manage a state-to-state relationship with President Mubarak as long as he protected the Camp David agreement while very quickly developing special relationships with the Muslim Brotherhood in Egypt and protecting them from criticism.

During those years when the Brotherhood was preparing to take over from Mubarak, I addressed Coptic American conferences in Congress several times and called on the U.S. government to respond to the attacks by Islamists and by the

Brotherhood on the Copts of Egypt as those attending these conferences were claiming. Neither the Obama-Biden administration nor the mainstream media supporting it (such as the *Washington Post*, the *New York Times*, and CNN) raised the issue of Coptic persecution in Egypt by the Brotherhood. The idea was that those claiming persecution by the Mubarak regime could not be persecuting the Christian communities of Egypt. Obviously, this was not true as the Copts have been presenting convincing evidence that Brotherhood militants were attacking them across Egypt while the Mubarak government was unwilling to protect this old minority. A number of members of Congress petitioned the State Department and the White House several times between 2009 and 2013 to raise the issue of minority protection in Egypt with Hosni Mubarak—without success. A partial reason for this lack of success was that the same Mubarak government was receiving pressure from the White House to not suppress the Brotherhood. So, it was impossible for the regime to be pressured by the U.S. administration to stop going after the Ikhwan while being pressured by the U.S. Congress to go after them because of persecution.

By the beginning of the Egyptian revolution of 2011, the State Department and democracy agencies, including the International Republican Institute and the National Democratic Institute, had already connected with the Egyptian opposition in general, but as we observed, they had built strong ties to the Muslim Brotherhood network at the expense of the Copts and Muslim moderates. Already, by the end of spring 2011, a number of members of Congress and European Parliament and I were expressing concerns over how the administration was navigating the Brotherhood groups in Egypt, putting pressure on the armed forces to allow these political networks to maneuver within the country in order to secure power through elections.

The majority of indications from January pointed toward civil society clearly desiring a non-Islamist state path after Mubarak, but the White House pressure split the Egyptian public into two blocs: one reminiscent of the Mubarak regime and the other simply rising against the latter. The Brotherhood was the most organized of this second bloc—as well as the most recognized by the international community, led by the United States—and positioned themselves as the leaders of the antiauthoritarian regime opposition that brought Mohamed Morsi to power.

The Brotherhood was in full control of Egypt from the end of 2011 and through the entirety of 2012. During the first six months of 2013, the Morsi regime showed signs of regional connections with Islamist and jihadist forces, sending serious evidence to Washington that the government of Egypt was leaning toward becoming more and more radical and suppressive of its own secular opposition. Morsi hosted several events, including a major rally in Cairo for a plethora of radical movements, such as Hamas, Islamic Jihad, even elements who would later become ISIS, and Ikhwan factions from around the world. Moreover, Morsi built strong ties to the AKP government of President Erdoğan in Turkey and a strategic alliance with the funder of the Brotherhood around the world, the emirate of Qatar.

By the spring of 2013, Egypt, under the Brotherhood, was coordinating regional activities aimed at bringing down the Saudi and UAE governments. My reading at the time was that Egypt could not have engaged in these activities with Islamists without at least a nod from the Obama-Biden administration.

Egypt is the best evidence of Obama—and the radical leftist policies of the Democratic Party—supporting Islamists over civil society, of supporting the enemies of freedom rather than the oppressed seeking freedom.

A solid core of liberal opposition to the Brotherhood was formed in Egypt, consisting mainly of journalists, lawyers, judges, students, artists, workers, and farmers who had participated in the first revolution of January 2011. That core tried to engage the Obama administration, complaining about the Brotherhood suppression, to no avail. The civil society opposition launched its own movement to remove Morsi without any international support, which was conveniently blocked by Washington.

At a Coptic conference held in Washington during the last week of June 2013, I met with representatives of the secular opposition of Egypt who informed us that a popular uprising was on its way. Indeed, one week later on June 30, 2013, thirty-three million Egyptians walked in massive demonstrations in Cairo and other major Egyptian cities demanding the resignation of Mohamed Morsi and the dismantling of his Islamist militias, who were responsible for violence against Egyptians in general and Copts in particular. Morsi, defiant and calling on his supporters for jihad, rejected the demand of the largest protest group in the history of the world and instead unleashed his militia against the protesters.

The protestors, with no international support as it was being blocked by the United States, called on the Egyptian army, which was mainly formed of conscripts and thus of and from the people, to help them against Morsi. General Abdel Fattah al-Sisi, minister of defense, then decided to side with the largest demonstration of protesters in the history of the world and ordered the arrest of Morsi and installed an interim cabinet made of bureaucrats until several referendums and legislative and presidential elections formed a new government in Egypt with new political bodies. The Obama administration called their revolution a military coup, ignoring the thirty-three million protesters and the support of an overwhelming majority of the ninety million Egyptians.

Egypt, with the largest Arabic population, had successfully ousted the authoritarian—and then ousted the totalitarian Muslim Brotherhood—without the help of the West, and in fact, in direct defiance of and in opposition to the goals of the Obama administration. The change in Egypt broke the backbone of government by the Muslim Brotherhood of North Africa. The 2013 revolution in Egypt impacted Tunisia and Libya where anti-Islamist uprisings had begun as well.

After the debacle of Egypt that summer of 2013, the

administration focused more on achieving the second leg of its grand strategy in the region, which was to negotiate with the Iranian leadership a deal that would end the state of enmity between Tehran and Washington and resolve a number of crises in the region from Iran to the Mediterranean sea. But the angle used by Washington to engage the Iranian regime over a possible agreement was not based on pressing Iran to pull its militias out of four Arab countries, freeing them; rather it was based on releasing frozen funds belonging to the Iranian people—to a regime on U.S. terror lists.

CHAPTER 7
OBAMA'S ISIS DEBACLE AND THE IRAN DEAL

The ISIS Debacle

Not winning a war of ideas against the jihadists will simply pave the way for the rise of another jihadist movement. That is what happened in Iraq. Even after the Bush administration's military surge between 2006 and 2008, the mission was left unfinished. In addition to removing the jihadists' military power, there needed to also be a victory in the war of ideas culminating in a partnership with Iraqi civil society to uproot the jihadists from the hearts and minds of the people. However, starting in 2009, the Obama administration began moving in an entirely different direction, abandoning the war of ideas, refusing to engage in counter-jihadism, and last but not least, remaining unwilling to partner with non-Islamist moderate Muslims across the region, even in Iraq.

Because the American people were growing weary of the war in Iraq, Obama had a winning talking point in the 2008 campaign, but the decision to withdraw from Iraq was not truly linked to the best interests of the American public. Not only did Obama abandon the War on Terror in spirit; the decision to withdraw from Iraq as soon as possible was indicative of Obama's desire to engage the Iranian leadership in negotiations for what would later become known as the Iran deal.

This piling up of strategic mistakes starting in 2009 led to the mother of mistakes at the end of 2011 when all forces were pulled out from Iraq as promised—without having real strategic partners on the ground, other than the Kurds in the north. Our friends in the Sunni and Shia communities were overwhelmed by the return and the expansion of pro-Iran Shia militias.

The political capital between the people of Iraq and the government of the United States dissolved. The takeover of areas evacuated by U.S. forces by Shia radical militias linked to Tehran was a direct cause for the alienation of the majority of Sunnis in Anbar, the Sunni Triangle, and other areas. For three years, the Iranian militia's separation of Sunni tribes and communities left deep scars among them. On the other hand, the lack of engagement by the U.S. with those Sunni moderates disabled them from confronting the rise of the Salafi extremists within their own ranks. Allowing Iranian militias to seize the country and abandoning Sunni moderates to vie by themselves against these militias and the jihadists was a perfect recipe for disaster.

A number of jihadi groupings formerly with al-Qaeda of Iraq gathered inside Syria and were able to start controlling some areas thanks to the Syrian civil war. They were successful because the U.S. was late in engaging civil society groups against Assad. The Islamists took over between the end of 2011 and early 2014, again because of a strategic failure in Syria in the early days of the uprising; the U.S. did not fully engage with the moderate elements of the Sunni majority against the Assad regime. The jihadists obliterated the moderate Sunni opposition and established bases in northwest and southwest Syria. The Kurds were trying to establish enclaves in the Northeast, racing with jihadists around them. In the center, jihadi elements from Iraq launched the Islamic State of Iraq and Syria.

ISIS gradually moved from its Syrian bases to Iraq after the U.S. withdrawal and as the Iranian militias were crushing the Sunnis of Iraq—the perfect storm allowing Daesh to seize as many Sunni areas as possible. Between June and August 2014, ISIS invaded almost every Sunni area of central and northern Iraq. ISIS committed horrendous massacres across the land among Arab Sunni tribes, Assyrian, Chaldean, and Syrian Christians, and the worst bloodshed was against the Yazidis with killings, abductions, and sexual slavery for women and children.

The massacres perpetrated by ISIS were a humanitarian disaster. The mass killing of the Yazidi community in the north was by far and proportionally the most horrendous of all. At the end of July 2014 I rushed with a delegation of NGOs to the United Nations Security Council and met with members and with the secretary-general's office, urging for a massive UN intervention to secure Sinjar and Nineveh, Yazidi and Christian territories, and establish an internationally recognized protective zone. Unfortunately, without a consensus between the United States and Russia because of the veto power they each have, it was impossible to create such an enclave for minorities. In Washington, I helped the Yazidi community engage with the administration, urging the White House to order air strikes against ISIS as it was seizing their villages and towns in the Sinjar province. The vital U.S. action came slow, late, and was not decisive.

Later, I reconstructed the situation and understood that the Obama administration was under two pressures to *not* intervene militarily, at least not decisively, at that time. One pressure was coming from the Brotherhood lobby, which advised avoiding having the Americans fight Islamists again and instead relying, eventually, on Qatar and Turkey to resolve the issue of ISIS, not Americans. On the other hand, and as dramatic, the White House was further engaged on a track of dialogue with Tehran and was thus not willing to clash with the Ayatollahs at a critical time. Iran did not want to replace ISIS with local moderate militias; it wanted its own militias to take over from the Sunni jihadists. This double attitude regarding the Brotherhood and the Iranians caused a delay in U.S. action, leading to a humanitarian disaster. It was five years later that the Trump administration ordered a very decisive takedown of ISIS.

In a nutshell, the choice to leave Iraq to Iran in return for reaching a deal with the Ayatollahs was detrimental to the peoples of the region and also to U.S. national security. We had to go back to Iraq and fight another war, a war that two administrations had already fought earlier, in order to shrink the new enemy. Hesitating and being slow to push back against the terrorist radical network due to pressures by the Muslim Brotherhood was also catastrophic on all levels.

2014 was not a good year for the United States in the Greater Middle East. We sided with the Brotherhood against a majority of Egyptians, sided with the Islamic militias in Libya instead of the elected parliament and its armed forces, sided with Nahda in Tunisia instead of the secular movements and women, and sided with the Islamist militias in northern Syria (yet at the same time we did not go all the way against the Assad regime with the administration and its seniors, such as CIA Director John Brennan, saying that reaching out to "the moderate wing" of Hezbollah was something we could do). In Iraq, we cooperated with the pro-Iran militias against ISIS while in Yemen we did not back the Saudi-Emirati alliance in their fight against the pro-Iranian Houthis. But the greatest bungle came at the end of 2014 with the decision to link up with the Iranian regime and sign the infamous Iran deal.

The Iran Deal

Lots of ink has been spent on the Iran deal debate over the past five years between the Obama camp and the Trump camp, but thanks to the media, the big picture remains unclear. Readers might be surprised to learn that the Iran deal, which Americans were led to believe was simply about curbing Iran nuclear ambitions through a return of offering incentives, was actually an economic transaction of epic proportions. Not only did it shift wealth from one world network to another, it gave the brokers of the deal access to immense profit from the dividends and the opportunity to establish a power system to manage a new regional and international order produced by that deal.

The Obama-Biden administration agreed to release $150 billion to the Iran regime— ostensibly in return for a commitment by Tehran to slow down and stop its pursuit of nuclear power. It appears that Iran used those funds, or at least parts of them, to invest in influence inside the United States to ensure the protection of that transaction (and future ones outside the frozen accounts). From that gigantic transfer of monies to the Ayatollahs there of course would be people who would profit from a return. The financial gains made by the regime would somehow directly or indirectly be shared with those who made it possible in the West and in the United States. In this way, the political machine that produced the Iran deal would one way or another also be strengthened by the deal it achieved. Thus, it would try to protect that transaction in a fierce way to ensure its long-term viability.

But there is more. Not only would influential circles in the West and in America profit from the central transaction of the $150 billion but also from new markets that would open up once the deal was signed and moving. These new markets included those of oil and gas from Iran as well as from areas controlled by the regime in the region, including Iraq, Syria, and Lebanon. Just imagine the combined energy resources stretching from Iran to Iraq to eastern Syria and to the Mediterranean—and remember that across from Syria and Lebanon under the sea lies one of the largest reserves of gas and oil yet to be extracted. That market is the ultimate prize of the Ayatollahs in Tehran, worth *trillions* of dollars. The import-export implications for the centralized countries should also be factored in.

Although money was the greatest incentive for the deal—as is almost always the case—was this really just a case of "follow the money" or "follow the power"?

The history of the so-called Iran deal is much older than the year it was negotiated and signed, 2015. The transaction reflected a much wider accord that was initially proposed by the leaders of the Islamic Republic after the collapse of the Soviet Union. The idea was that the rulers of the Khomeinist regime in Tehran were ready to exchange their stabilization of violence in the region for hundreds of billions of dollars, which were frozen in American and other accounts around the world after the takeover by Ayatollah Khamenei in 1979 and the multiple terror attacks that took place in the 1980s and early nineties. The Islamists of Iran were trying to legitimize their control of one of the most important oil-producing countries while still waging terror in the region and around the world. They were looking for a U.S. administration that would accept such a deal, but mainstream America leaders, Democrats and Republicans alike, had consistently rejected such an offer for decades.

Iran and its agencies remained on the U.S. sanctions lists for many years. From Clinton to George Bush, the post-Soviet era did not see a reintegration of the Islamic Republic into the international community because of its enmity to many nations, including the United States, Israel, and a number of Arab countries. However, the Iranian leadership designed a new strategy based on recruiting radicals in the West, from both the Right and the Left, to advance their influence as a way to lobby for the integration in the world economy they so desired. Hence, we saw Far Right neo-fascists siding with Iran and the Assad regime of Syria against Israel based on antisemitism. And we also saw Far Left neo-Bolsheviks becoming defenders of the Iranian regime. But it was through the latter group, meaning the left wing in the West and specifically in the United States, that Tehran was able to score significant influence.

After the collapse of the Soviet Union, Communists around the world split into two factions. One faction tried to survive as a self-sustained Marxist movement opposed to all fundamentalist forces from all backgrounds, including the Islamists. And the other faction of neo-Marxists decided to work with Islamists, seeing them as a social force they could use to defeat modern-day capitalism. In America, Far Left activists and intellectuals followed the second school of neo-Marxism, joining the Islamists' struggle, using them as a tool to recover power.

In America, the left wing also was splitting between the traditional liberal and social Democrat Left and the neo-Marxist factions now described as "Far Left." While the traditional Left, after the fashion of Joe Lieberman and Tom Lantos, remained loyal to prevalent mainstream foreign policy regarding the containment of Iran and pushing back against the Salafists, the Far Left clearly moved to form an axis with the radical forces in the Middle East, such as that with the Iran regime and the Islamists. The Obama group of radical leftists and left-wing campus networks converged with Middle East radicals. The Far Left, Islamic radicals, and a regime that for decades has been an official terror threat joined forces. The Far Left and the Islamists successfully formed a powerful alliance when Obama ascended to the presidency. And it was out of that womb that the Iran deal was born.

And the Iranian regime has been active in attempting to destabilize the Shia areas of eastern Saudi Arabia and Bahrain in order to one day control them, which would give them control over large volumes of Saudi oil and Bahrain's energy reserves. The rulers of modern-day Persia have an empire in mind that would control a huge segment of the world production of energy, oil, and gas. But to control it they need to seize the territories where those reserves and production facilities are situated, thus the Iranian strategy of penetrating Iraq, Syria, and Lebanon and destabilizing Eastern Arabia and Bahrain. And we can further understand why Iran got involved in Yemen via its Houthi allies. This offensive aims at encircling Saudi Arabia to destabilize it and launch Iranian control over its eastern provinces.

So if a regional power like Iran can gain control over a whole chunk of the Middle East, it could then open these titanic markets to its partners in the West who provided, via the Iran deal, protection of the regime. If America opposes Iran's ambitions in the region, all these goals will be jeopardized, but if Washington indirectly releases the Iranian regime to accomplish this geopolitical objective, the rulers of Iran could invite their partners both in Europe and the United States to be part of this historic venture. From that strategic perception one can understand the true depths of the Iran deal.

This mother of all deals between the Iran regime and Western partners to create a joint venture could ultimately become the largest, richest deal ever, dwarfing the wealth of modern China. So once the Obama administration started to engage in negotiations with the Iranians, neither side was actually looking to resolve a nuclear problem per se, but to achieve great wealth and power.

The irony, perhaps, is that each side of this deeper, greater, and much more serious deal believed they had the upper hand in the equation. Iranian leaders thought they were using an American administration dreaming of left-wing designs and surrounded by high financiers planning on aggrandizing their wealth—and that at the end of the day, Iran would emerge much stronger and push back against what they perceived as a bourgeois and weak-minded Washington. The Obama administration and its financial allies thought the converse. They believed that they could bribe the Ayatollahs with the Iran deal and that eventually the economic elites would stop Iranian ambitions on a geopolitical level and transform them into an economic partnership. The naive liberal and progressive elites of America believed they were playing games with the rulers of one of the oldest countries in the Middle East—the one that invented chess.

Iran Uses the Deal to Expand

Taking advantage of the negotiations, Iran started a quick expansion program in the region starting in 2014. First, Shia militias inserted themselves into the fight against ISIS across Iraq. As talks were progressing, so were Iranian militias on the ground. Prior to the ISIS blitzkrieg in Iraq and Syria, pro-Iran militias in both countries had secured the ground and were supporting Assad in Damascus and the Maliki government in Baghdad. When the jihadi network seized large segments of Iraq, the Hashd militias pulled out and then came back behind U.S. forces, Kurds, and regular Iraqi troops to seize the areas liberated from ISIS. American troops did not oppose the return of Shia militias because of the commitment of Washington to the talks with Iran.

In Lebanon, Hezbollah expanded unchecked by the U.S. As for Yemen, Houthi militias were on the offensive against that government and the Saudis while the Obama team was pressuring the latter to accept a negotiated solution, which meant that Washington protected the procuring militia in Sanaa from the pressures of Yemenis and labor UAE.

In sum, Washington's Iran policy allowed Iran to expand.

In 2014, in preparation for the finalization of the talks, the Obama-Biden administration sent $1.4 billion to the Iranian regime. Tehran used much of that money to beef up its propaganda machine in the region and within the West.

On July 14, 2015, in sharp opposition from many members of the U.S. Congress and the Senate, the Iran deal was signed between Iran and the P5+1 (five permanent members of the UN Security Council—and Germany).

As I watched the reactions across America, very few people understood the larger aim of the deal, and the so-called mainstream media provided all the rationale to smooth out its perception by citizens. The equation that was affirmed (it was either the deal or war) was obviously not reality. The real equation was: Surrender to Iran or work with the Iranian people to correct the policies of their government.

But the White House had no intention of listening to the concerns of the critics within the United States nor those in the region. By the end of 2015, the agreement with Iran was in full force and the partnership with the Muslim Brotherhood was maintained.

CHAPTER 8

THE EMERGENCE OF DONALD TRUMP

The Donald Trump I knew before 2015, and the one I have been familiar with since my days in Beirut, was the VIP who shaped the news of the entertainment industry and was on the covers of magazines and front-page news from New York to around the world. He was the fascinating representative of an American culture that was liberal, open, and artistic. He was a rough New York businessman whose competition often ended up in court battles.

To those of us who lived overseas before our emigration to this unique country, Donald Trump was part of the same world of famous icons as Jacki-O, the Prince of Monaco, or the British royal family—at least in the press. But the builder of the Trump Tower on Fifth Avenue in Manhattan had an additional layer of social impact on world leaders and normal people around the globe even in the eighties. His lightning success in the world economic capital of New York City and the speed with which he became one of the most powerful businessmen in the most powerful democracy on Earth gave birth to many an optimistic ideal.

Like Reagan, who came from Hollywood, Trump came from outside politics but had charisma like Kennedy, who was a politician with a life fascinating to the social public. He had a vision for America and a vision for himself as a president. And you could see the frustration in his eyes that he had no power to rectify what he saw as wrong with his own motherland. There was an urgent fire in his belly.

When Donald Trump started making political statements, first on Fox News, where he appeared frequently with the channel's top journalists, he demonstrated knowledge on economic and financial policies. I observed him more after 9/11 and noticed how uneasy he was about the prosecution of the War on Terror under Bush, and then I saw him fiercely opposing Barack Obama. By 2012, during the Romney campaign, he endorsed the Republican candidate and was later blasted by Obama at the White House Correspondents' Dinner. Slowly, Trump drifted away from the art and financial elites. Perhaps he was mentally preparing to take on a new challenge.

I believe Trump decided to run for the presidency after the defeat of Romney. He realized in 2008 with the defeat of McCain that no Republican candidate could defeat the Obama machine. He was probably right. The last candidate who was sophisticated enough to face off against that machine was, in fact, Romney. But in retrospect Romney's own political machine, a much more traditional one, never had a chance. The landscape of elections and mobilization shifted entirely after the Obama phenomenon rose in the country. The Democratic Party had a more organized and militant network of activists backed by the majority of mainstream media outlets. That machine was also prone to win the electoral battles because Republican leadership never caught up even though its base, moving harder to the Right in a spurt of passion against the Obama regime, delivered one final victory in the legislative elections of 2010.

What made a Donald Trump candidacy possible was his sixth sense, which informed him that a strong (and large) undercurrent was expanding out of frustration with the eight years of the Obama presidency. And, as Donald Trump himself said, the Republican Party was like a vehicle he could drive to victory, adding his own skills and his ability to connect with a wider and uninterested base.

By the time the New York tycoon announced his candidacy in Manhattan at the Trump Tower in June 2015, he had not yet announced any foreign policy except the broad principles he supported, such as ending excessive financial aid to other countries and controlling the borders. He did, however, appear to be a determined candidate with a greater self-confidence than I saw in any of the other candidates. This may have been because he was part of New York's business wars that are, in fact, as lethal and stressful as outright national politics.

Over the summer of 2015, I didn't hear much from candidate Trump on national security and foreign policy, other than focusing on the border situation with Mexico and on ending foreign wars, two concepts that became very popular with a large segment of the American public because of the mismanagement of foreign policy by the Obama administration and because of the poor results, at least as perceived by the public because of media opposition of the Bush interventions in the region.

The New York businessman had strong instincts to his advantage. He opposed the wrong choices of the Obama administration, and he opposed the bad implementation of the Bush administration's policies. But he had one more advantage, which was his connection to a large segment of the silent majority of the least politicized section of society.

Trump the candidate criticized all foreign policies after Ronald Reagan. The latter's vision was one of defense and national security under the tough conditions of the Cold War. The economic life of American businesses during the confrontation between the United States and the Soviet Union necessitated a clear and strong response to the Communist bloc. Such a vision survived the Cold War and was naturally adopted and simplified after 9/11. Like the common American, Donald Trump was questioning the political establishment about why the wars against the terrorists were not won. It was as simple as that. Hence his war attitude was not about being defeated or tired or unwilling to confront, but (as I understood it) simply to win wars and not get entangled in them.

Another characteristic of the candidate observable during the six months of his 2015 campaign was the clear ability to understand the collective feeling and sense of a large portion of American citizens who were fed up with the old ways and who were overwhelmed by the Far Left ideological warfare. Trump connected with the popular base, but more importantly, the latter connected with him.

As I observed Mr. Trump when he spoke to rallies, I became more and more convinced that the Republicans needed a leader who would be able to mobilize the masses much more effectively than previous presidential candidates, including Senator John McCain and Governor Mitt Romney, understanding that the Republican campaign in general was facing a very powerful Democratic machine backed by a very astute president who had the long experience of political organization, which I personally saw in action during the 2012 campaign.

Obama would be backing Hillary Clinton in November 2016, which meant it was his platform that would be adopted by the Democratic candidates, along with his strategies, his resources, and his unique organizational tactics. Add to the mix a mainstream media which had built a thick-as-thieves relationship with the White House for the past eight years. I saw the Obama machine at work in 2011 and 2012. I had closely observed the Obama foreign policy agenda for almost a decade, and I had felt the brunt of media campaigns targeting me. I personally experienced in U.S. politics how a Far Left ally to Islamist movements can wreak havoc not just for a presidential campaign adviser but also tarnish the image of a presidential candidate himself or herself.

The urgency of choosing a candidate who could mobilize voters upset all other parameters. In my view, neither America nor many regions in the world could afford another four or eight years of an indirect third or fourth Obama term. In short, my strategic calculations and my experience in social and political mobilization over several presidential election cycles told me that if the Republicans did not put forward a super candidate, undaunted and relentless, they were going to lose again. Donald Trump had precisely the tools necessary to face off with an incredibly powerful machine backed by an incumbent with eight years in the White House and the vast resources of government.

For Trump, not coming from the political world was an advantage because not only did this resonate with the American people, but his strong outsider personality would not allow the factions within the Republican Party that had held Romney back in 2012 to create the same inertia in his own campaign.

CHAPTER 9

TRUMP VS. OBAMA—THE CAMPAIGNS' FOREIGN POLICY POSITIONS

The April Mayflower Foreign Policy Speech

On April 27, 2016, the campaign organized a major event with the media and diplomats featuring a speech by candidate Trump about his views on foreign policy. In my view, this was the launching pad for what would become the Trump foreign policy doctrine at its first stage. It would impact the foreign policy direction for the campaign, the transition, and, more importantly, the actual foreign policy of the Trump administration. In that speech, Trump outlined major strategic directions for which many in the conservative and right-of-center base decided to vote on national security grounds. One main direction was his opposition to the Iranian regime expansion in the region. And in my view, the one statement he made that changed the landscape of the race, especially with the opposing camp that the Obama-Biden administration was behind, was his declaration that he would not accept the Iran deal. In my view, that was his crossing of the Rubicon, after which he would incur heavy attacks by the supporters of the deal and those who had been and would be profiting from it.

Trump also committed to a confrontation with the radical Islamists, including ISIS, al-Qaeda, and all sorts of jihadists. He also pushed back against the Muslim Brotherhood and was very clear when it came to what he called extreme vetting in finding better countermeasures to the infiltration by jihadists into the U.S. homeland. The speech also covered the major points of the Trump platform, including his position on China, immigration, bringing the troops home, and more. All of his major policies were in line with varied Republican and conservative agendas, but two of the policies made all the difference to me because they would need super effort in order to be executed. One was withdrawing from the Iran deal and the other was freeing Washington from the Brotherhood influence. And these two voiced policies were exactly the reasons why both the pro-Iran lobby and the pro-Ikhwan lobby went after the Trump campaign and later, of course, the Trump administration—each lobby from a different angle.

Arab Coalition

Another signature policy goal that Donald Trump promoted during the campaign was the formation of an Arab coalition that would confront the terrorists in the region and back the international coalition against ISIS and the Iranian regime. I had been calling for an Arab coalition or an Arab "NATO" since 2010. I suggested it to the Romney campaign in 2012, but it was Donald Trump who welcomed the concept and made it a plank in his Middle East platform. The candidate looked at it from a financial perspective first. It was logical for Mr. Trump that the regional coalition would foot the bill of activities in the Middle East to push back against the radicals because the countries were large oil and energy producers.

While George Bush (41) had formed coalitions including Arab countries to repel Saddam Hussein's forces from Kuwait in 1991, and while George Bush (43) also included Arab and Muslim countries in the U.S.-led campaign in Afghanistan in 2001, the Obama administration did not opt for an official alliance of Arab countries to push back against the jihadists and Iran for the simple reason that his administration was seeking a deal with Iran and therefore would not gather Arab allies against the regime in Tehran. It is also important to remember that the Obama White House was mostly active with Islamist movements across the region by backing their drive to seize power in several Arab countries such as Egypt, Libya, and Tunisia, via "self-styled revolutions," and eventually increase their influence in the Gulf and in Syria. Therefore, the Obama administration did not form an Arab coalition against the Islamic State and jihadists because it was seeking a future coalition of Arab countries under the leadership of the Muslim Brotherhood. Trump proposed the opposite. He opposed the Iran deal, committed to fight the Islamists, and proposed a logical tool, an Arab coalition.

The War against ISIS

Another signature policy of candidate Donald Trump during his campaign was a commitment to wage a full systematic war to stop ISIS from expanding, reverse its rule in Iraq and Syria, crush the caliphate, and dismantle it. The Obama-Clinton platform also committed to fight ISIS in Syria and Iraq. The administration had already begun (starting in 2014) to wage air sorties against the jihadi network. But there was a major difference between Trump and Obama-Clinton regarding ISIS, which was the speed with which the caliphate had to be dismantled. Between 2014 and the end of 2016, the Obama administration instructed the Pentagon and other agencies to keep the White House appraised of almost every move, including the tactical ones, so that the advisers could match them with diplomatic efforts and negotiations for the post-ISIS decline. In practicality, this meant that Washington was coordinating its military efforts with other players in the region, indirectly with Iran in the Iraqi government and directly with Turkey.

Because the administration was in a negotiating mode with Iran over the Iran deal in 2013 and 2014, the Obama administration allowed the pro-Iranian militias to advance on the ground while U.S. air assets were striking at ISIS. They did not want to jeopardize the talks and later the actual deal by fighting against ISIS on the one hand and blocking Iran allies from seizing the ground on the other hand. Which explained why the U.S. campaign against ISIS stretched from August 2014 until December 2016 without a major shift on the ground. Iran did not want large numbers of U.S. troops operating in Iraq or even in Syria, and they also did not want Kurds in either country, or moderate Sunnis, to be the ones seizing territory. It was comparable, though not identical, to what happened during World War II when the allies allowed the Soviets to take territories from the Nazis in order to apply the Yalta agreement.

The other factor that slowed down the Obama administration's offenses against ISIS was pressure from Turkey and the Muslim Brotherhood, which was maneuvering to try to replace ISIS with Ikhwan Sunni militias, mostly in Syria but possibly in Iraq should conditions favor it. The Muslim Brotherhood and the AKP government of President Erdoğan also wanted to inherit the space occupied by ISIS in Syria. And both forces were putting tremendous pressure on the administration in order to be able to seize the Syrian zone of ISIS. However, what blocked them was geography, and the Kurdish forces of the SDF (who were in conflict with Ankara as well) were the ones gaining control of the lost ISIS zones. The U.S. military, for practical reasons on the ground, gradually allied itself with the Kurds and other minorities, which allowed them to seize territory instead of the Islamist militias.

In addition, there were some leftist elements in the circles of the Obama administration who wanted the YPG in northeast Syria to gain influence, which meant that the Obama administration dealt with Iran, Turkey, and the YPG at the same time as it was putting pressure on ISIS. Too many regional and local politics were involved in the campaign against ISIS, but during the spring and summer of 2016, candidate Trump was committing to waging a relentless campaign against ISIS—the fastest possible, so that it wouldn't recruit tens of thousands of more jihadists and eventually send them to other countries, including to Europe and eventually to the United States. The difference between the two campaigns regarding the fight against ISIS was not in the principle, which was adopted by both, but in the strategies— where one campaign and the administration behind it had other deals with other factions on the ground which delayed and stretched the operations on the ground, versus the Trump campaign which, though never experienced in managing state military affairs, was yet committed to do the job faster and regardless of any other sub-deal.

Middle East Minorities

Donald Trump was very clear in his call to stop the persecution of minorities in general and of the Christians in the Middle East and North Africa. His particular interest in making the protection of endangered communities in the Middle East a U.S. policy came from his friendship with the very active evangelical community in this regard. His campaign was initially able to garner support from conservatives partially because of the bridge he built to that question for an American bloc of about 60 million people across the nation. Politically, this open call to protect communities which have been attacked, massacred, ethnically cleansed, and suppressed for years provided Mr. Trump with automatic support among millions of church-going Christians across the country.

The concept became real after many leaders observed the concerns of average Americans via their church leaders about the atrocities committed first by al-Qaeda and then ISIS, across Syria, Iraq, and other countries, particularly between 2014 and 2016.

Candidate Trump's platform spelled hope for a new U.S. policy of protection to all minorities, not just Christians but also Muslims who were targeted by jihadists. If Donald Trump became the president of the United States, he could help these minorities and civil societies stand on their feet and be secure. In contrast, the Obama-Biden administration and the Clinton-Kerry State Department had completely ignored and then abandoned the very concept of small minorities struggling for their freedoms in the Arab Muslim world.

There was a political explanation for this abandonment. Since the administration had cut deals with the Iran regime and the Muslim Brotherhood, it refrained from backing Christian, Yazidi, and Bahá'í communities so that they would not alienate their regional partners. This was also true with regard to the abandonment by the Obama White House of so many civil societies in the region as well as secular and liberal dissidents, for the same reason.

The Iranian Green Revolution was ignored, Iranian dissidents were dismissed, and Copts from Egypt, Assyrians, Chaldeans and Syriacs, Kurds, African people from Darfur, and many other minorities were all complaining to us in Washington and in Europe about how distant the Obama administration had become since its inception in 2009. The bottom line was that a Trump administration, even if we had no idea whether it would commit or not, was—by far—a much better option than what we had experienced with the Obama administration regarding the question of minorities in the Greater Middle East and Africa.

Candidate Trump on Immigration and Refugees

Among the easier talking points used by Trump was the border question, known broadly in America as "the wall." This point electrified millions of voters who felt less safe, especially during the eight years of the Obama administration, which had opened the borders to a strong and steady flow of illegal migrants. A large segment of American society did not feel comfortable with this de facto change of demographics and cultural identity.

The second "easy" talking point by the candidate was about migration and refugees. Here again Trump expressed what a large segment of public opinion desired to see: not a stop to migration as his political enemies often charged, but regulation of the flow, better organization, and, above all, a vetting of the people coming into the country. This point was so logical that I could not understand what the Left was complaining about. Yes, America is a country made of immigrants (I am one of them), but what does that make Canada, and practically the entire Latin American subcontinent? Yes, millions of immigrants cross the Atlantic—and some the Pacific—to join younger countries that were settled at the expense of the native tribes in the Americas. This is part of the history of the Americas in general and of the United States in particular, but it is the tip of the iceberg of the great movement of populations that has taken place around the globe on all continents. People move. The entire planet has been subjected to migrating hordes, then tribes, then nations and empires. The Western Hemisphere has had a slightly different history of migration simply because of geography. It was separated from the Old World by immense oceans, and no one in American politics argued against receiving immigrants to add to the population. The only difference was that the public opinion within conservative America, and even people in the center, wanted to regulate that movement of population. The Obama administration, for eight years, seemed to have opened the valves in a way that caused politicization of a traditionally widely held position.

The United States includes a rich history of extending a hand to those fleeing for security and freedom, absorbing them, and transforming them into citizens as part of the collective psyche of Americans. But the Obama administration manipulated this historic tradition to specifically target elements belonging to radical factions and bring them in to use them as propagandist militants both inside the United States and overseas.

It was no problem for the Obama White House to bring in large numbers of individuals affiliated with the Muslim Brotherhood or those close to the Iranian regime or other radicals. And as I discovered in over twenty years as an expert on political asylum with U.S. immigration courts, the actual victims of the Middle East were often rejected by the administration and their causes ridiculed by the media allies of the Obama camp. Muslim Brotherhood activists were welcomed. Coptic Christians and Lebanese opponents to the Syrian occupation or Kurds, let alone individuals from Darfur, were having a hard time coming to the United States between 2009 and 2016. The situation worsened greatly under Obama because of the removal of expert material from the FBI, CIA, DHS, State Department, DOJ, and various military agencies, material that would have helped the government identify the jihadist ideology and therefore the political asylum seekers or refugees—in order to filter out the radical elements and those who committed jihadism. It would be the equivalent, and I underline again the *equivalent*, of allowing committed national socialists to freely enter the United States during the 1930s or World War II while rejecting the applications of Jews and other communities persecuted by the Nazis.

And then there was the question of refugees from war zones. In my comprehensive meeting with the candidate back in December of 2015, I gave the idea of safe zones specifically in

Syria. The concept was geopolitical as refugees have nowhere else to go and they were surrounded by dangerous forces about to obliterate them, the next neighbors were under the obligation to receive them, and the United Nations was under the obligation to care for them and manage them until a solution to their problem was found. Hence, in Syria, there was an opportunity to establish safety zones *inside the country*: to receive refugees, host them, and protect them until a solution was found. And when that was not possible, and time did not allow, those refugees crossed the borders to Turkey, Lebanon, and Jordan and found refuge. Obviously, the UN and international humanitarian organizations are supposed to be tending to these refugees either inside safe zones within their own countries or in the adjacent neighboring countries.

The Obama-Biden administration was, however, proceeding in some strange direction. They were planning on uprooting those refugees from their ancestral lands in Syria or in their immediate refuges in neighboring countries and flying them all the way to mainland United States. Nobody questioned Washington on why the administration chose to do this. This was baffling because Syrian refugees' first base instinct reaction, especially among women and children and the elderly, was to return home to their neighborhoods and their villages.

The Endless Wars

One of the most famous slogans produced by the Trump

campaign, and actually used often by the candidate himself, was the goal to end all endless wars and bring the troops back home. This was not a real innovation in terms of American political thought. Since before World War I, U.S. leaders have been swinging between what was known as isolationism and interventionism, a see-saw between Americans willing to intervene overseas in defense of American interests and Americans focused inward and rejecting any meddling around the world, especially in long, protracted conflicts. We see that debate prior to World War I, and then the U.S. came back into isolationism in the 1920s. We saw it again in the buildup to and our entrance into World War II. The U.S. insisted on staying neutral in European and other conflicts until after the Pearl Harbor attack when the American public then endorsed entering the war in France. Again, that dichotomy manifested itself during the Cold War as the U.S. confronted the Soviets and engaged in several regional conflicts such as in Korea and Vietnam, and then the Gulf War as well as the Afghanistan and Iraq wars. Throughout a full century, the U.S. was swinging between intervening and not, entering wars or refraining.

Donald Trump was a very international businessman with connections to VIPs and politicians around the world, and thus was not and is not an isolationist from an academic and political perspective. Isolationists refer to doctrines or to nationalist economics as their ideologies. However, the then-candidate made a strategic political choice to call for the principle of putting America first. But this was in the sense of organizing priorities, not transforming the country into an inward-looking social group.

Like every campaign, the Trump campaign could be seen as a very large umbrella. It included a wide variety of opinions, some of which were authentic classical isolationist views similar to the agendas of post-World War I or post-Cold War advocates. But we also had those who were reacting to interventionism worldwide as excessive, expensive, and going in the wrong direction. Moreover, politicly, Mr. Trump, who is very well connected to the collective sense of the lower middle class, the largest social group in the country, also realized that after eight years of Obama's so-called "interventionism" and concessions to actors around the world, including Iran, China, Russia, and the European Union—as well as his friendships with Far Left forces in Latin America— the slogan "America First" would go over intensely well with his base.

NATO

As of his first foreign policy addresses, candidate Trump criticized NATO for not meeting its financial obligations and leaving the U.S. to foot the bill by itself. This approach pleased the large patriotic base of Donald Trump, just on its principle. Many Americans who had been frustrated with Obama's policies—and even partly with Bush's policies—rallied to the Republican candidate's frustration with allies who were not meeting their obligations. However, in my view, and in addition to the financial snag, there were larger strategic problems with

NATO's bureaucracy. The Western alliance, which did well during the Cold War, has not been focused enough since 2001 on the actual central threat. First, its actions, outside Afghanistan where it performed well, did not match the seriousness of the jihadi and Iranian threats worldwide. In Libya, the U.S.-led NATO campaign removed Gaddafi but allowed jihadists to take over. Regarding Iran, NATO sat idle while the U.S. was confronting the threat alone. NATO moves to contain Russia on its eastern border weren't very successful nor fast enough. Trump wanted a full reform on financial grounds, but the real reform had to be strategic, as I tried to argue.

Other Foreign Policy Choices during the Campaign (Asia and Mexico)

China was definitely high on the Trump campaign's agenda and very personal to the candidate. Donald Trump seemed to have thought deeply about how to handle China-U.S. economic and financial competition. He was in the field, though in the private sector, and appeared knowledgeable about both crunching numbers and trade relations between Washington and Beijing. The candidate's major goal regarding relations with China was to rebalance the financial and economic ties between the two countries. He was critical of the Obama-Kerry approaches to China, which Trump described as weak. Trump's position did not depart from the mainstream Republican position in regard to China. He believed, like many around him, that it was the Clinton administration that brought China to the world financial structure via the World Trade Organization, and the U.S. industrial sector that invested in China because of the cheap labor. Trump blamed both the Democrat establishment and the capitalist network which allowed China to gain the upper hand in the economic relationship because of the spending of America and Chinese control over huge levels of debt to the detriment of the American worker, as he described it.

China feared a stronger leadership in Washington, and Taiwan hoped for a Trump escalation against China and therefore opening on the island nation.

East Asia was also present in the campaign foreign policy narrative, but from a negative perspective. Mr. Trump put pressure on Japan and South Korea to pay their dues in return for American protection, as he called it. And Asian media was eager to know about Trump's position with regard to North Korea, with some of this media seeing a deal between the New York super entrepreneur and Chairman Kim. I was certain that the U.S. posture under Trump would actually be stronger, which we later saw when he sent the task forces to deter North Korea from firing missiles towards the United States.

Then there were the very public uproars by the Clinton campaign and other critics of Donald Trump regarding his remarks about the borders with Mexico and the famous slogan he used, "Mexico will pay for the wall." We were in a presidential campaign, and Mr. Trump had to develop a policy that would calm the fears of many Americans seeing the border disappearing and a series of waves bringing in very large numbers of illegal immigrants, basically refugees, who would not register and instead disseminate and spread across the country. That was a clear concept that Donald Trump brought into his campaign, and he mobilized his voters precisely because of it. It was night and day compared to the Clinton campaign's calls to open the borders to what they called unregistered or undocumented immigrants.

Trump responded with his unequivocal position to shut down the border, build a wall, and create a legal process to take place at the well-administered gates. He wanted immigrants. He did not want what he called demographic invasion. Trump was not anti-minorities. There was no indication of anything of the sort in his speeches, and nothing in the narrative within the campaign that looked anything close to the anti-immigrant narrative seen from the Far Right in Europe.

On ethnic identities Donald Trump was neutral. He wanted to see an Americanization of the migrants and the immigrants, which, ironically, is exactly what those immigrants want when they head toward America. People come for different reasons, mostly economic, but also for religious freedom, political freedom, peace of mind, or simply due attraction to a fantastic system of governance and culture. Trump wanted all that, like many presidents throughout a full century, but he wanted immigration to be organized. There was nothing in his public life, maybe not even in his private life, before becoming a politician that demonstrated any ideological or ethnic discontent with the multiethnic identity of this country. Hence, when it came to the southern border, the illegal migrants and refugees and the country of Mexico and the other Latin American countries, Trump was focusing on how to protect the stability of the homeland, not displaying an attitude toward other people's cultures. The only difference is that, unlike other politicians from both parties, he was frank and brutal about it, in contrast to other politicians who said one thing and felt the other.

INTERLUDE

Already, the reader should be able to see the stark difference between Obama's policies, which he had eight years to implement and solidify, and the developing policy agendas of candidate Trump. This is vital because when Trump went up against Hillary Clinton, it was, essentially, Trump's alternate view—not just in regards to domestic policy (which Americans seemed determined to focus on) but also foreign policy and, importantly, national security—and Clinton's Obama 2.0 agenda, a continuation of policies that emboldened jihadists and attempted to leverage relations with the Muslim Brotherhood and profit from dealing with the terrorist regimes of Iran and Venezuela.

This is important to note because as we enter the 2020 elections, the equation is quite similar. Trump has had only four years to reverse the policies of the Obama-Biden administration, all while under severe domestic political pressures—and again faces the Obama 2.0 foreign policy agenda that cares little about national security as he fights for another term against Joe Biden, Obama's own vice president.

There may be those who argue, however, that Trump was unable to accomplish all his promises, to undo everything that had to be undone, that he never quite made the right partnerships and that perhaps he did not go far enough in reversing the Far Left agenda in either domestic or foreign affairs. The reality, however, was that the opposition made it nearly impossible to accomplish anything significant in Trump's first term—yet Trump still accomplished much.

The opposition started undermining the legitimacy of the presidency from before the inauguration, and then ramped up its efforts at resistance to slow down any accomplishments that might be made by the Trump presidency.

CHAPTER 10
WHY A "RESISTANCE" TO TRUMP

Let's Start with Russia

The American public has, for four years, been submitted to a deluge of accusations and counter-accusations about Russian meddling in the 2016 elections, a saga that led to years of a judicial probe, further deteriorating relationships between political parties and within the American society.

Although I definitely saw signs of Russian attempts to manipulate and influence supporters of Mr. Trump across the country via posts on the internet and aired statements on Russian network RT, I never saw any direct strategic collaboration between the leaders of the Trump campaign and the Kremlin.

However, in my view, the most important factor was to understand U.S. relations with Russia as they were explained and devised by the leadership of the Trump campaign. The campaign policy regarding future relations with Russia on behalf of the United States was very simple to understand. Donald Trump and his team clearly put the defense and the national security of the United States above all considerations regarding any foreign power. There was nothing grayish about that position. I would even say the Trump position with regard to Russia (in my view) was clearer than the Obama-Clinton view of their position with regard to Moscow.

While we all remember President Obama challenging presidential candidate Romney in 2012 during the debate, accusing the Republican candidate of still living in the Cold War just because Mitt Romney told him that Russia is a "geopolitical foe," Obama looked at Romney as though he was an alarmist simply because he said we should pay attention to Russia's strategic activities. Later, President Obama doubled down by telling President Medvedev to relate to Prime Minister Putin "to be patient" with Obama until he is re-elected ("after November"), meaning the then-U.S. president desired very friendly relations with Moscow but had to lower the volume of that narrative because he was facing an election with a conservative candidate who seemed to be tougher on Russia. Ironically, the Clinton campaign blasted Trump in 2016 for being Russia-friendly even though Secretary Clinton in a very memorable moment presented Russian Foreign Minister Sergey Lavrov with a reset button in Moscow.

The bottom line was that Trump was resetting U.S. relations

with Russia to move from being afraid of Moscow and servicing its leadership from a lower position. He wanted to bring the U.S. back to a higher position, to correct the relationship and move it from "tense and unequal" (with the U.S. at a disadvantage) to "equal and relaxed." Besides, Russia had moved from being the Soviet Union to a nationalist country moving towards different manifestations of balance of power.

The Putin leadership wanted to reaffirm the national borders of the Russian state and thus engaged in tensions with several of its neighbors—in the Caucasus with Ukraine and in the Baltics. The Obama administration, as we saw in 2014 during the invasion of Crimea, did not do much to try to resolve those issues. It started to talk tough about Russia only when Donald Trump started to propose a different policy, one that appeared to be more rational, actually, than the fluid Obama-Clinton-Kerry maneuvers.

The Trump agenda first wanted to signify to Moscow that America would be developing a mighty military to protect itself, protect its allies, and make peace—a bit like the Kennedy and Reagan doctrines. But the Trump attitude was that there are areas, such as in Syria or against terrorism or even in space, where Russian-American cooperation is possible and desirable, including, obviously, in the never-ending search for denuclearization.

There was, however, no secret plot between the candidate and the Russians. There may have been activists within the campaign who for various reasons favored stronger relations between the

U.S. and Russia, and some of these voices were heard loud and clear, including among lawmakers such as former presidential candidate Senator Rand Paul and California Congressman Dana Rohrabacher. Ironically, those who favored better relations between Washington and Moscow were found in the campaigns of both parties—and for years. Actually, there were and are more lawmakers in the Democrat Party inclined to favor that line than in the Republican Party as it was clear in the narrative of presidential candidate Congresswoman Tulsi Gabbard and years ago Senator Sanders, who vocally supported better relations with the Soviet Union.

The Russian matter was also spread by those in Europe who had been supporting the Iran deal because of deep financial interests. The European partners in the Iran deal and the companies that would make huge money out of entering the Iranian market were furious at Trump because of his stated intention of withdrawal from the deal. It appears the pro-Russia story was circulated by the anti-Trump networks out of Washington, and maybe behind them by the bureaucracy of Barack Obama. That became clear to me when, during debates, some European politicians said they felt closer to the Clinton campaign and to the Obama administration rather than to the Republican Donald Trump. Later on, the same panel said that the main achievement of the Obama-Kerry team was to produce the Iran deal, which was great to them. Eureka. So, indeed, it was about the financial bridge between Tehran and Brussels, and that bridge all the way to Washington. Donald Trump was stepping into a river of interests, triggering a tsunami of anger across, mainly, Western Europe.

But at the time of the convention in 2016 I did not realize or even imagine for a second that the Obama-Biden administration would be monitoring the campaign, spying on some of its leaders, and as we learned in 2020, engaging in intelligence manipulation against one of the two major political parties of the United States. That was completely beyond any imagination, including a story line in the most fertile of political thrillers.

Unfortunately, the opposing campaign and administration then, and later the Democrat opposition, portrayed a false description of the Trump attitude towards Russia, creating one of the most serious challenges to American stability, and at some points even challenging the integrity of our national security.

The Battle of the Media

During the Romney campaign, and before that, during the McCain campaign in 2008, the media was up in arms, abandoning its neutral reporting position and adopting a totally partisan attitude. But during the presidential election cycle of 2016, that same media leapt from partisan to political enemy of Donald Trump. Something big must have happened for the American media to become, in many instances, complicit or comparable in its systematic attacks against the candidate to a point where it wasn't even debating substance but instead following the path of petty smear.

Often, the defenders of Trump would rely on one simple explanation: "They hate Trump." I believed it was more than just simple hatred. Donald Trump willingly or unwillingly had stepped over a vital resource for the opposition, and the opposition was fighting with all they had to stop him from getting to the White House. The media's behavior was a representation of the camp that was going after the candidate. My hunch was that the matter was not just about domestic politics, but it must be an issue of foreign policy.

The pre-election resistance, I believe, simply came about because the Trump team was serious about containing Iran and dismantling ISIS and was considering changing the Obama apology policy regarding the radical Islamists and the Brotherhood.

Islamophobia

Since the controversial statement made by candidate Trump during the fall of 2015 about allegedly shutting down Muslim immigration to the United States, and the way it was understood by the Left and the critics of Mr. Trump, global media aimed for the Republican candidate, accusing him of Islamophobia and "racism." Trump's base understood his tweets and statements as they were intended—as the people were also concerned that a mass of refugees could be infiltrated by radical Islamists coming from so-called Muslim-majority countries, and never saw his position as a systematic rejection of any visitor or refugee based simply or solely on his or her religion. Mr. Trump wanted to shut down Islamist penetration of the country, and he used "Muslim," instead of "Muslim Brotherhood." But in the heat of a campaign, his opposition did not do him the favor of giving him a chance to explain even though he had experts, speechwriters, and eventually supporters from the Muslim communities. In fact, there were NGOs and community leaders and activists from the Arab Middle Eastern and Muslim communities in the United States who actually understood what Trump meant and were looking forward to becoming community and media surrogates to push back against the charge of Islamophobia. They launched the American Middle East Coalition for Trump to respond to the extremists hijacking of the message of these communities.

The reach of the AMCT widened to include almost all communities from Iran, Sudan, and Turkey to Arabs, Jews, and Berbers. The group rose in defense not just of the candidate, but of the platform, and dug in deeper, counterarguing against the pro-Iran and pro-Brotherhood activists working within the other campaign. The coalition was noticed by the media, by the Clinton campaign, by the Obama administration, and, as importantly, by civil societies across the Middle East. Just a few months after Donald Trump was accused of so-called Islamophobia, he had a wide coalition of Muslims and Middle Easterners coming to his defense. More notably, perhaps, some Muslim religious leaders opposed to the jihadists appeared at Trump rallies, and on Election Day, experts estimate that in Michigan and in Ohio the coalition was able to muster proportionally significant numbers of votes to secure those two states.

Obama Exit Strategy

Traditionally, when a candidate is elected president in the United States, as of the moment the results have become official, the president-elect becomes the legitimate near-future leader, meaning he and his team become the leadership of the nation that is in charge of directing the policies to begin officially as of January 20. There are some consequences that have been sacred since this constitutional process was established. First, the incumbent administration should cease any commitment to engage the future of the United States both domestically and internationally. Because an American majority has chosen a new president and entrusted him or her with the direction of the country, the incumbent becomes a caretaker of national security and foreign policy in addition to domestic issues. The incumbent no longer negotiates for new policies. The administration manages the national security matters day to day and starts transferring these matters until the elected president and his or her administration officially enter the White House. And secondly, the incoming administration, the transition, should not manage the current and ongoing executive steps as it cannot sign a document, issue orders, or mobilize troops. But it *can* talk to future teams. It can discuss world affairs with world leaders, enlighten them on the policies that they are going to follow, and clarify the differences with current policies if they do exist. Foreign leaders and governments should be briefed very clearly on what the transition is planning on doing so no chaos ensues during the transition. The incumbent White House and its executive agencies should not interfere with the preparation work of the incoming administration. And the incoming administration should not in practice interfere with the day-to-day policy.

This understanding has worked for centuries and is well understood by the guardians of the institutions. In fact, it is taught in colleges and understood by the public. However, the transition between the Obama and the Trump administrations was an exception because the departing power had interfered in the work of the transition, specifically on national security and foreign policy levels.

The first sign of obstruction against the incoming Trump administration occurred when, in January 2017, we heard of news concerning General Michael Flynn. This was very strange news, saying the national security adviser was speaking with the Russian ambassador about a possible future lifting of sanctions and about suggesting ideas about a matter related to Egypt and Israel and the Security Council of the UN. The news reports said FBI agents interviewed Flynn about this conversation while writers in the media mentioned the Logan Act! I had a hard time understanding how the Logan Act applied, or even why General Flynn was interviewed. It is normal for an incoming administration to be in communication with foreign countries, especially with large powers, as the transition is winding down. As I argued earlier, incoming presidents have the obligation to be in touch with the international leaders as they are being familiarized with various dossiers, including the ongoing crises.

So when a transition national security adviser, in this case General Flynn, was speaking with a foreign ambassador about matters that a Trump administration would be handling a few days later, the Obama administration should not have been sending the FBI or any agency to interrogate the top level advisor on national security of the incoming government about these matters. Flynn was speaking with the Russian ambassador about sanctions and about a vote at the Security Council. The Logan Act was designed to prevent American citizens, mostly abroad, from organizing joint action with foreign governments by claiming that they are the sitting administration of the United States. That was absolutely not the case in the Flynn situation. He never claimed he was the sitting administration, Russian authorities knew he was in the transition, and there was no executive coordination with the Russians before January 20. It was not about a violation of the Logan Act. It was about preparing for further action by the Obama bureaucracy while power shifted to the Trump administration, precisely because of a disagreement on several points of foreign policy. An action that would hurt the national security process of the United States for the following three years.

CHAPTER 11

THE BATTLE OF OBSTRUCTION VS. TRUMP

The First Offensive by the Opposition

By the end of December 2016, all seemed to be smoothly moving towards establishing the Trump administration and launching its various projects in foreign policy and national security. Among the first initiatives that it planned to immediately initiate was a withdrawal from the Iran deal and the formation of a large Arab and possibly Muslim coalition to assist in fighting the terrorists and pushing back against Iran. Another immediate goal was to beef up U.S. presence in the Middle East to strike at the ISIS caliphate, both in Iraq and in Syria, and eliminate the physical presence of this jihadi network that was brutalizing the populations and threatening international security. Last but not least, in the Greater Middle East, the Trump White House was contemplating a new initiative to give rebirth to the peace plans between Israel and the Palestinians. Jared Kushner was given leadership on producing what was then called the deal of the century. And several other tracks that were set up during the campaign and the transition would also lead to official international goals.

Rex Tillerson was named as the first secretary of state of the Trump administration, in from the world of business and oil, in order to set up a new system of communications with world leaders, many of whom he had met or had exchanges with as CEO of ExxonMobil. General Mattis, coming from the Marines, took the helm of the Pentagon in order to coordinate the counterattack on ISIS and the restructuring and renewing of all United States Armed Forces. The Trump apparatus was ready to move forward on all these tracks. General Flynn was to coordinate the networks of U.S. power to achieve these goals. And this is where the first strike against Trump came like a bulldozer.

General Flynn appeared at the podium of the White House in January 2017 and issued a very stern warning to Iran signaling the forthcoming Trump administration campaign leading to the withdrawal from the Iran deal and the formation of an Arab coalition. The White House was positioning itself to begin with new policy designed during the campaign and it was unfolding in those first few days of the administration. A few days later, a probe targeted the first national security adviser of the Trump administration, paralyzed him, accused him of wrongdoing, and forced the president to remove him amidst a media bombardment backed by the opposition in the U.S. House of Representatives against the advisor. The top man of the Trump offensive was taken out.

In that part of January, President Trump and his team did not yet understand the scope of the political and legal offensive waged against them through a breach by the bureaucratic opposition at the Department of Justice. The only loss the president felt was the resignation of General Flynn, which would also have a tremendous cost in the prosecution of national security policies. This would lead to at least two years of slowdown and paralysis. Half of the Trump presidency was taken out via the removal of the central adviser who had the trust of the president in national security matters, among all other political advisers. This created a huge hole in the White House when it came to national security planning and strategizing. The Iran deal would have to wait for another two years.

Trump's First Counterstrike

On April 7, 2017, Donald Trump surprised everybody, including me, when he ordered missile strikes against an air base under the Assad regime in retaliation for an alleged chemical attack by the regime against its opposition. Even now, we don't really know the circumstances or motivations behind that order. What we do know is that Trump did what Obama failed to do previously: cross the red line in Syria and strike at the heart of the regime. Some explained that such a strike would eliminate the opposition's argument that the president was too close to the Russians. An attack on a base where Russians operated would have disproven those talking points. Another argument was made that Trump was showing his intention to pull out from the Iranian nuclear deal by hitting at the Assad regime, ally to Tehran. No matter what the reasons were, the new White House successfully performed a U-turn in policy from that of the Obama White House in terms of showing a willingness to confront Iran.

Going on the Offensive: The Riyadh Summit

The summit in Riyadh took place in May 2017. It was an excellent opportunity to showcase U.S. leadership and engagement with the Arab and Muslim world, a very necessary image for pushing back against the president's so-called Islamophobia. Besides, his new friends from the Arab world, namely President Sisi of Egypt, Mohammed bin Zayed of the UAE, and Mohammed bin Salman of Saudi Arabia, as well as others, had been preparing for just such a grandiose event since the end of the presidential campaign. The removal of Flynn did not impact the holding of the summit but did slow down the global U.S. strategy against the Iranian regime.

The U.S. summit with the Arab and Muslim world held in Riyadh was a historic display of a new strategy bringing America to the heart of the Middle East as Donald Trump addressed more than fifty leaders on the necessity of driving the radical forces out, crushing the ISIS caliphate, pushing back against the Iranian expansion, and waging a relentless war of ideas against radicalization and indoctrination by the jihadi ideology.

The summit by itself was a smashing success. In a sense, it was a response to the Obama speech in Cairo in 2009 and a redress of the U.S. policy that not only brought the Iran deal but allowed—if not aided—the Muslim Brotherhood in their quest for power across the region during the Arab Spring. As I was watching the unfolding of the summit with all the players I'd had in mind since the beginning of the decade, including Egypt, Saudi Arabia, the UAE, Bahrain, Jordan, Morocco, and others, I believed that the Trump administration was able to reposition itself in the right direction and even in a better, larger, and more determined way than during the last year of the Bush administration.

The summit also led to three major strategic decisions crucial to reversing Obama's policies. One was a full-fledged containment policy regarding the Iranian regime expansion, leading eventually to the dismantlement of the Iran deal and restructuring security in the region. The second was a renewed effort and backing of a U.S. campaign to remove the ISIS caliphate from Syria and Iraq and go after the terrorist cells in a joint effort in the region and worldwide. For that purpose, it was decided that a joint Arab-Muslim force, à la NATO, of about thirty-five thousand troops would be formed and put at the service of the Arab coalition to intervene wherever it is needed to implement the two principles. The third and probably most important decision made by the summit that would affect the region for the long term was to push against the ideologies that produced terrorists and the so-called Khomeinist revolution. This counter-extremist center was to be established in Saudi Arabia, a historic move since many had for years criticized the radical circles within the kingdom for being behind the spread of the radical ideology. But it was only possible when then-deputy crown prince Mohammed bin Salman took it on. Along with UAE leader Mohammed bin Zayed and Egypt's Sisi, MBS waged a global/regional effort to isolate the influence of the Muslim Brotherhood around the region. Hence, the summit was a successful achievement by the Trump administration to contain and reverse the two most dangerous extremist menaces in the region, Iran and the Jihadists-Islamists (ISIS militarily and Ikhwan ideologically).

The ISIS Strategy

The United States deployed in Iraq and Syria, and the Pentagon was instructed by President Trump to go ahead and use all resources possible to eliminate the jihadist army. There was no need for other players to authorize the policy. Even the Iraqi government, which was under the influence of Iran, did not oppose U.S. action on the ground. Trump's war on ISIS was seen as beneficial to all players threatened by the jihadi network; hence there was no serious opposition to the U.S. military spending American dollars to crush the terrorists. In fact, those bodies on the ground—including the Iranian-backed militia in Iraq, the Iranian regime, and the pro-Iran circles in the United States—did not give the White House a hard time in this regard. Their real goal was to replace ISIS with forces sympathetic to Tehran. In other words, the Obama bureaucrats did not oppose the military action that would eliminate one force if another pro-Iranian force could take over while waiting for full restoration of the Iran deal.

However, the bureaucratic opposition to the Trump White House, along with the Democrat opposition in the House of Representatives, under the heavy firepower of the so-called mainstream media, blocked the two other policies and pinned down the administration for almost two years.

The joint influence of the Iran lobby and the Muslim Brotherhood fiercely opposed Trump action, first to remove the Iran deal and second to put heavy pressure on the regime. A collapse of regime would mean the crumbling of the Iran deal, and therefore all interests linked to it. The Muslim Brotherhood, mostly backed by Qatar, opposed the other policy launch by Trump at the Riyadh summit, which was to counter the ideology of the Islamists, which would eventually block the Muslim Brotherhood from expanding their influence in the region and beyond. It was important to divert attention from these foreign policies, either through advising against pursuing them or crippling the power of the presidency. The opposition was committed to effectively ending the goals that would undermine the policies of the Obama administration.

The Mueller Probe

The administration prepared to take the first major step in launching the so-called Arab coalition. A date was announced for May 20–21, 2017. Stunningly, pro-Obama bureaucrats, in coordination with opposition lawmakers, launched the Mueller probe on May 17, accusing the president and his orbit of collaboration with the Russian leadership! Though it may never be proven that the timing was intentional, there can be no mistake in reading the move as a strategic interception of the Trump drive to launch an Arab coalition with partners opposed to both Iran and the Muslim Brotherhood as such an initiative would serve as a platform from which to bring down the Iran deal and break apart that U.S. partnership.

The launching of the Mueller probe against Trump and his associates did not deter the president from launching the Arab coalition. This crossroads was a make-or-break moment for Donald Trump policy in the Greater Middle East, the major battlefield where he could prove American leadership, which could then be taken in all directions, towards Europe, NATO, China, and Venezuela. Its completion would reverse Obama's Middle East policies in one shot, raise an Arab coalition from the dust, signal a counteroffensive on Iran as well as on ISIS, and eventually revive the peace process.

From the end of 2016 into winter 2017, the narrative of a so-called Russian influence and/or meddling into the 2016 elections was taking a different direction than a normal inquiry by governments in general, and the Department of Justice in particular, of illegal activities by foreign countries in our electoral system. Had the issue been a web of technical activities, such as online hacking and/or social media manipulation or even illegal payments made in order to further the candidacy of local, national, or even presidential elections, then this would have been a usual law enforcement operation to bust such crimes. American politics has always known election troubles. This was not new territory. But what was in the works during 2016, revealed in early 2017, and became a matter of national security was not those usual illicit activities.

The bureaucracy of a previous administration, the one that just exited, including national security and intelligence agencies, was involved in spying on an opposing campaign and then moved to try to crumble a duly elected president and his administration, not just because of political differences, but because of a drive to protect political agendas that were designed by that exiting administration with a high likelihood that those interests were not just American interests.

In 2016–2017, the actions of the Obama-Biden administration and then its bureaucracy were not about the law and how and whether or not it was breached. It was about paralyzing the Trump administration using the full power of politicized national security and intelligence agencies. This had never before happened in American history. While the pro-Trump camp and the Republican Party and its base were shocked to see a part of the government trying to dismantle the other part to protect political interests developed during the previous administration, it was more than a personal attack. This was the antithesis of a liberal democracy. What was worse than this drama was the width and depth of the parts of the bureaucracy involved in this attempt to bring down a president and his administration. His administration endured bureaucratic machination lasting more than two years. Two positions that exist in order to protect national security and law were disabled and failed to protect the state from its own unelected bureaucracy: the national security advisor and the attorney general.

It was clear that the new national security adviser, General McMaster, had shown no interest, as far as we saw in his public statements and actions, in strong counter-strategic movements to contain the Iran regime expansion based on the Trump agenda and the resolution of the Riyadh summit. McMaster, according to his team, also downplayed the indoctrination role played by the Muslim Brotherhood and thus did not develop a strategy to counter it. President Trump was deprived from within his own national security team of impetus and strategies to face off with the two main menaces. On top of that, when the congressional inquiries started about the so-called Russian conspiracy with the Trump team, the president's own attorney general recused himself in a ridiculous way, claiming that he had reasons to do so. In fact, he did not. He was just afraid of what he did not know. Without an attorney general to assist him, President Trump relied on his own lawyers in the White House. He left the Department of Justice to the opposition to be used against him and his administration. With AG Sessions removing himself from defending the national security of the country, his deputy Mr. Rosenstein appointed former FBI director Robert Mueller as a special counsel to investigate the alleged Russia-Trump connection and refer it to the DOJ for prosecution.

It was as if the opposition split into three armies. One started with the Democrat opposition group in the U.S. House of Representatives, which initiated the complaint about a so-called conspiracy between Donald Trump and the Kremlin, which was by itself an outlandish, dangerous, and destructive allegation. That group petitioned the Department of Justice and pressured the AG to recuse himself. The whip was in the hands of bureaucrats who were part of the efforts to remove Trump. That was the second group inside, the DOJ. Then, within the appointments of the Mueller team, a third group was formed of prosecutors mostly from the opposition. This means that the operation to stop President Trump from proceeding with his national and foreign policy included lawmakers, DOJ bureaucrats, and a probe. And all three were backed by a very aggressive media. Basically, the political opposition had landed inside the state bureaucracy and was conducting an effort to remove the president or stop him from implementing his policies.

Never in American history, let alone in the modern era of Western liberal democracies, has such a set-up taken place. The oldest similar kangaroo court in Europe took place in France under the infamous "Dreyfus affair." Using the security agencies and the justice system to change foreign policies and remove elected leaders was never a feature of advanced liberal democracies.

There were many devastating results of "Russia-gate." First, this was a national trauma. Across the country, people suddenly felt insecure and disoriented after their president was falsely accused of being an agent of a foreign power. That alone will need decades to heal. Second, because the White House was targeted by prosecutors and massively shelled by a hostile media collaborating with the probe, national and international policies of the administration were affected and slowed down. With no AG to bust the conspiracy and a national security adviser unfocused on the two main threats emanating from the Middle East, the president had to slow down on removing the Iran deal and change direction on removing the influence of the Muslim Brotherhood within the United States and worldwide.

The Qatar Nexus

In mid-June, four Arab allies to the United States who were part of the Riyadh summit decided to follow what they thought was a call by President Trump to drive extremism out of the region. They organized a boycott of the principality of Qatar, asserting that the regime was supporting the jihadists in multiple spots in the region, backing the Islamists and working to topple the governments of moderate Arab countries. Saudi Arabia, the United Arab Emirates, Egypt, and Bahrain cut relations with Qatar and stopped communications between their countries and the Ikhwan world base in Doha.

Turkey and international Islamic networks sided with Qatar while secular and moderate Arabs and Muslims sided with the Arab coalition.

In the United States, the choice should have been crystal clear, for Doha had been intensively active, not only in backing jihadists and Islamists, but also for years, specifically since 1997, waging vicious campaigns against the United States, particularly through its media platform Al Jazeera. The principality had become the headquarters of the international Muslim Brotherhood network, and for years it had funded them and sheltered them.

Evidence abounds supporting the idea that Qatar has been behind the radicalization of Islamist networks throughout the Middle East, around the world, and even here in the United States. Not only is Al Jazeera its media arm, but I and other experts understand from that evidence that Qatar and the Brotherhood and their extensions within the AKP government in Turkey have been at the center of a global network of Islamists and jihadists.

But Doha developed a mighty lobbying force in Washington, D.C., protecting the influence of Qatar within both parties. The pressure group peaked in influence under the Obama administration and maintained a level of influence under the Trump-Pence administration. Though the Arab coalition that initiated the isolation of Qatar was in line with President Trump's speech and his insistence that the extremists should be pushed against, the reaction from Washington was lukewarm. To the surprise of the Arab coalition and of the lawmakers and experts who were actually waiting to see an action coming from the Arabs themselves to contain extremists, the administration did not support that move, and eventually Secretary of State Tillerson positioned himself as a mediator to resolve the problems between the Arab coalition and Doha and did not put pressure on the latter to reform, but put pressure on the Arab coalition to lift the embargo.

In my view, something went wrong in Washington when it came to the U.S. position regarding the Brotherhood, Qatar, and the AKP of Turkey. Unlike with Iran, the Trump administration did not want to open a front with the leadership of Doha and of the Muslim Brotherhood, despite the fact that Riyadh had purchased military materiel from the U.S. for more than $120 billion—versus Doha, which purchased around $14 billion worth. If the matter was just sheer commercial interests, Trump should have chosen the Arab coalition position, but it looked like the White House preferred to stay in the middle and manage the crisis from afar instead of meddling directly.

By the end of June, early July 2017, the immense pressure put on the Trump White House by the Mueller probe, the House opposition group of lawmakers, and the so-called mainstream media was able to cut down the energy Trump had gained from the Riyadh summit. Many in the media were asking me why the White House was slowing down on two strategic tracks in foreign policy, the Iran deal and the Muslim Brotherhood, despite the fact that President Trump had the full support of most of the Arab countries and Israel. The question then became who was threatening the president and with what.

Probe Escalates

The Mueller probe was an emanation from the DOJ, but a department that was politicized by the opposition. The main line of accusation against the Trump administration and campaign was about a national security matter, linked to a foreign policy dossier. The alleged charge was that Russia and the leadership of a campaign, thus of a main political party, had linked up to try to win an election, and then to coordinate policies. At first glance, this is something I might think is happening in Iran where the Pasdaran, the Revolutionary Guard, is trying to bring down a president just elected by the Green Revolution, charging him of being an agent to Israel. The scenarios are almost identical. Or maybe liken it to a security apparatus in a Latin American country sabotaging an elected president and accusing him of being an agent of the U.S. or Cuba. Stories you only see in movies. But sadly, it was not a Hollywood plotline.

The various committees overseeing the drama, in both houses and from both parties, tilted toward accusing the president of betrayal, even the Republican majority. There was something odd that bound politicians from both parties against Trump. There was an interest cementing them together. The questions I had included: "What is the deep interest driving the removal of Trump with such urgency? What was he doing to harm these interests?" The Intelligence Committee in the House of Representatives chaired by Congressman Devin Nunes was the heart of the Inquisition targeting the White House. Ironically, it was the Minority leaders who were leading the charge, including Congressman Adam Schiff.

Probe Pressure on Foreign Policy

By the summer of 2017 and going into the fall, the pressure coming from the Mueller probe had reached an apex, forcing the Trump administration to dedicate more time and effort to protect its own people and the president and ensure an efficient defense, leaving lots of space for the bureaucracies and foreign lobbies to press on their issues overseas. The Arab coalition emanating from the Riyadh summit was out there alone, facing multiple fronts, including the war in Yemen, the situation in Syria and Iraq, the Iranian pressures, and a growing political-diplomatic war with Qatar.

When the Trump administration, under immense pressure by the probe and the political forces both domestic and foreign behind the probe, failed to support the Arab coalition in its drive to isolate Qatar and force it to abandon its partnership with the Muslim Brotherhood and let go of its support to jihadists, the leaders of the four Arab countries, who were key allies of the Trump administration and his own partners in the Riyadh summit, decided to move forward without the U.S. umbrella. The UAE and Saudi Arabia escalated their campaign against the pro-Iran militias in Yemen without expressed and direct support from the White House. This allowed pro-Qatar and pro-Iran lobbies in Washington the strike they needed against the kingdom and the Emirates.

At several locations and for the following three years, members of Congress, and at times bureaucrats in the administration, threatened the Arab alliance with sanctions if it continued to pursue its campaign against the pro-Iran militias in Yemen. In Syria and Iraq, the Trump administration was prosecuting the war on ISIS systematically, but the opposition maneuvered to safeguard the Iran deal as long as possible. In Libya, the situation by 2017 was clear—the LNA on the one hand and the Muslim Brotherhood on the other. But that wasn't what the Obama bureaucrats were pushing in the Trump administration. Across the oceans, the crisis with North Korea was brewing, the situation with China was unclear, and the chaos in Venezuela was expanding.

Across the pond, tensions between NATO members and the Trump administration were surfacing. The rest of the world was seeking decisive moves by Washington, yet the probe and the opposition made it difficult. But not impossible. The Trump White House, at the peak of the Mueller probe pressures, maintained the new direction of its foreign policy but slowed down on the speed. The blurriness regarding the relationship with the intelligence community created hesitations at the level of decision-making nationwide. From what transpired in the public eye, people did not know who was backing whom and who was feeding the press about what. The remainder of the fall witnessed severe pressures from the probe and its allies throughout the bureaucracy and in Congress against the president and his team.

Kirkuk Crisis

During the fall of 2017, and while the probe was reaching its apex in Washington, a crisis in the Middle East that October would put even more pressure on the Trump administration in the midst of a severe domestic crisis. The Kurdish regional government in northern Iraq had decided to organize a referendum to decide if it would push for self-determination and independence (as many ethnic groups have done throughout history) or remain associated with the central authority in Baghdad, which was basically influenced by the Iranian regime.

The leader of the KRG, Masoud Barzani, had committed to the referendum and to move forward towards independence. The feelings of the Kurdish leadership and population were that the United States and international public opinion would eventually side with them because of the suffering of the Kurds and specifically because of the contribution of Kurdish military in the campaign against ISIS. During the U.S.-led offensive against the jihadi militia in Iraq, the most reliable fighters were those from Iraqi Kurdistan. Kurds and other ethnic minorities in the area felt that they had the same chance the Jewish nationalist movement had in British-mandated Palestine to create the state of Israel.

Kurds and minorities suffered genocide and at the same time struggled alongside the allies and felt that they deserved a homeland of their own. The Kurdish leadership in Irbil wanted to include the city of Kirkuk, which had a Kurdish majority but also included Arab Sunnis and Christians as well as a few Shia neighborhoods. Historically, the city was Kurdish and Christian, but demographics evolved into a multiethnic society.

Since the downfall of Saddam Hussein and again after ISIS took over and the city was recovered by the Peshmerga, the military forces of the KRG controlled the city. The latter assumed that the United States, which was pounding ISIS and whose president had committed to supporting and arming the Kurds since the campaign, would allow the Kurds to keep Kirkuk under their control and eventually include it in the referendum on self-determination. But Kirkuk is the center of a significant territory which has extended oil fields. Add to that how the Baghdad government led by Prime Minister Maliki was aligned on Iran policy and thus wanted to control Kirkuk via the popular mobilization units known as Hashd Shaabi, and a standoff between the Peshmerga and the Hashd took place in and around the city with the pro-Iranians threatening to invade the city by military means.

The Kurdish leadership, which had been successful in organizing the referendum earlier and obtained a large yes in response to self-determination, turned to Washington for support. Alas for the Kurds, President Trump and his team were under heavy pressure by the probe in the media on the one hand and the national security adviser on the other hand, after Flynn did not support the cause. There were too many financial interests involved in the matter, including U.S. companies which had been contracted by the Iraqi government for a long time and in turn had weight in Washington, D.C., with the bureaucracy.

Iran Deal Battle

During most of 2017, and as President Trump and his team were facing huge domestic pressure, attempts to address the Iran deal slowed down and, in some ways, came to a complete standstill. In Europe, NATO partners were putting pressure on the new administration, calling on President Trump not to cancel U.S. participation in the deal. Within the bloc of U.S. bureaucrats, academia, and media there were calls to do the same. Obama supporters across Washington were organizing a resistance to the withdrawal from the JCPOA, but it seemed to me that there must be a link between this pressure and the extreme pressure from the probe on the Russian matter in order to disable the White House from opening a new front against the Iran deal. The absence of General Flynn and of other advisers who were the tough core during the campaign was felt at the White House. Add to that the resignation of two more advisers who worked on strategic planning, Steve Bannon and Dr. Sebastian Gorka. The time between the end of 2017 and January 2018 was the hardest timeframe for Trump foreign policy.

Last but not least, the bureaucrats from the Obama era were still committed to the Iran deal and therefore sided with the Iraqi government and pro-Iran militias instead of the Kurds. The latter were left to vie for their own interests.

In the end, Barzani resigned and his local government let go of Kirkuk. The Iraqi Kurdistan remained isolated by the Iraqi government for a while, with all flights from the outside world shut down, forcing the population to take flights through Baghdad in order to get to Kurdish towns. It was a setback to Kurdish independence, but also somehow an emotional weakening of special U.S.-Kurdish relations in Iraq. This was due to the fact that the probe had again pressured the White House to a point of imbalance between Baghdad and Irbil. Kurdish autonomy was still guaranteed by the U.S., but Kurdish independence no longer was, thanks to the influence of the Iran deal.

CHAPTER 12

THE ENDLESS CHAIN
OF CHALLENGES

The harvest of 2017 was clear. President Trump formed his cabinet and national security team amidst a fierce launch of a massive investigation against his administration in a manner that had never been done before. While his goal since the campaign was to change the direction in foreign policy and national security and, of course, in domestic and economic policies as well, his first year, like all of his years at the White House, was a struggle on two fronts. One was to defend himself, the White House, and the administration from the tactics of the Russia investigation. And the other front was to advance his agenda with great difficulties because of the resistance, the most powerful of which being inside the bureaucracies of his own administration. He scored points on all fronts but was delayed in moving forward. From the Arab coalition summit in Riyadh to the recognition of Jerusalem as the capital of Israel, the White House tried to secure the minimum base from the initial campaign agenda while ensuring power and stability—the greatest challenge any U.S. restoration had confronted since the Civil War.

Venezuela

There was another crisis brewing in the southern part of the hemisphere in Venezuela where a Far Left regime, heir to anti-America and pro-Iran president Chávez, was suppressing its own population and opposing American influence in general and particularly the anti-communist drive by the Trump administration. President Maduro, seizing the opportunity that Washington was in turmoil internally, clamped down on the demonstrators between December and January. But U.S. policy had to make a U-turn from the Obama years, which opened widely to Cuba, Nicaragua, and Venezuela, ending the travel ban to Havana and trying rapprochement, first with Chávez, and then Maduro.

China

Trump's major challenge in the field of international economics was to find new ground rules for the relationship with China. He convinced a large segment of the American public that a change should occur. America, since the 1990s and under the auspices of the Clinton administration, had facilitated the integration of that Communist government into the World Trade Organization and thus into the world markets. American companies have since migrated to China, developed a web of production and interests, and eventually trained that giant country to adapt to the capitalist system worldwide. Since 9/11, while the United States was busy with several wars, China was leaping economically to a point where it was serving as a cash bank for the United States and many other countries. During the Obama years, Beijing rapidly expanded in all confidence from Asia and Africa to Latin America, building a vast network of trade and export. Washington was borrowing dizzying amounts of cash to continue with its programs, but a subdued relationship was built between a Communist ruling class and business elite in China, and the United States was exhausted by its domestic and international obligations. President Obama chose the strategy of further integrating China in world forums of the economy, hoping that would change the behavior of the regime. Trump rejected this approach and upon arrival at the White House designed a different strategy: putting open political pressure on Beijing, establishing personal relations with Chairman Xi, and reclaiming America's financial independence from China's juggernaut.

Southern Border Crisis

Migrant and refugee issues are not usually seen as national security matters but matters of immigration, legal or not. But during the summer of 2018, it was a different story. U.S. and Latin America-based militant networks organized long convoys of refugees brought from Central America, including from Guatemala and El Salvador, as well as from countries overseas.

These were all organized by an international network on the Far Left with extremist connections. The convoys of busses and cars were formed by militant volunteers connected to groups operating within the United States. The goal of Operation Refugees was to transfer large masses of civilians penetrated by militant networks and hit the Mexican/American border over and over to overwhelm immigration security, enter the U.S. territory, and then disperse and disappear inside the American population.

There were two objectives for the mass urban move. One was to get waves of populations from Central and Latin America illegally inside the United States, but the other was to put the homeland at the mercy of radicals. Two years later during the summer of 2020, the answer to the enigma transpired. The possible hidden agenda of the penetration operation, in addition to increasing the voting power of one party, was to use these groups with no legal status and no financial capability as foot soldiers in the urban riots across the country, including in Portland, Seattle, New York, and other cities.

The network behind the organized transfer of population into the U.S. homeland was part of the urban resistance against the Trump administration and in general terms against the U.S. government. But there was another agenda for this hazardous mass travel with women, children, and the elderly. It was to push civilian populations in distress to try to cross the border everywhere they could, even under physical danger, just to produce the breakdown of the southern border—putting the blame on U.S. guards, Border Patrol, and, of course, the ICE agents. A general crumbling of the U.S. border with Mexico would then bring a mass exodus from the population, an expansion of the cartels, and in all this chaos, they could blame the Trump administration for it. The media was on the side of the militant organizers, already blaming the White House for "putting women and children in cages and ruthless mistreatment of refugees." This is a classical tactic by radicals in this hemisphere, but also in the Middle East. The crisis was real, and it became one of national security—first, because of the violence involved, and second, because of an attempt to dismantle the border with the consequences attached to that.

The Trump administration, still confronted with endless legal action coming from the probe and Congress simultaneously, took the political hits before it reorganized itself and enabled DHS to act swiftly but humanely. The situation stretched on for weeks, but it was brought under control by the end of the year.

Midterms: The Opposition Wins

The midterm elections were won on November 6, 2018, by the Democrat opposition. The House of Representatives was controlled by a majority from the Democratic Party, led by a returning Speaker Nancy Pelosi, an ally of former president Obama. But a new group was the most radical wing of the opposition and included what was known as "The Squad," comprised of newly elected representatives Alexandria Ocasio-

Cortez of New York, Ilhan Omar of Minnesota, Ayanna Pressley of Massachusetts, and Rashida Tlaib of Michigan. The group was a new, powerful player in the Washington political field. The midterm elections results put an end to the already precarious cooperation between the U.S. House and the White House, especially on foreign policy and national security. The new House majority was expected to turn against the president when its term officially began in January 2019. For the next two years there would be a major clash between the opposition's majority in the House and the presidency while the Senate was a battlefield between a slight Republican majority and a hostile and vocal Democrat minority.

The Super Impeachment

The Mueller probe consumed two and a half years, ending in March 2019. It split the country in two, spread uncertainty, and dragged the national security bureaucracy into unprecedented politicization, harvesting a lack of trust from the public. It did not reach conclusions that would remove the president from the White House, but still left major damages within Trump circles. But although it delayed major foreign policy decisions and projects, it did not eventually stop them. Trump then gained about six months within which to move forward. That was not enough time before a second hit came from the opposition, this time well positioned in the second branch of government, Congress. President Trump was in the position of former president Obama after the midterm elections of 2010 (split majorities in Congress)—with one difference: a domestic and an internal pressure on the administration's institutions from the bureaucracies.

On October 31, 2019, the opposition majority in the U.S. House of Representatives launched the impeachment process alleging that President Trump, while on an official international call with the president of Ukraine, made illegal demands from his counterpart. The tenor of the conversation heard by many of us officials and by several agencies who usually listen to the conversations was leaked to the opposition group in charge of the Intelligence and Judiciary Committee inside the House. Similar to the Russian investigation, the opposition alleged that the president used the conversation to score advantages for his campaign and against his opponent. The investigation, hearings, and impeachment vote seemed to score a complete loss until February, generating a similar impact on both domestic and international policies of the government. The White House again had to redeploy its resources to focus on the impeachment because the goal of any impeachment is to remove the president from the White House. Although his policy agenda came to a halt temporarily, a removal from office would have put a permanent halt to that agenda.

CHAPTER 13

TRUMP FOREIGN POLICY WARS AND WINS

Significance of the Iran Deal

Perhaps the single most important foreign policy goal on strategic levels in 2018 was President Trump's decision to withdraw the United States from the Iran nuclear deal. And an immediate corollary was the decision to put the Iran Revolutionary Guard on U.S. terror lists in the fall.

The Trump decision to end the Iran deal in 2018 was perhaps the most important of all decisions in foreign policy and in national security of his entire first term. In fact, it is the linchpin of Washington's challenges with the Middle East and international relations in general in this decade. The JCPOA was not just another deal with another country; it was a multilateral agreement involving the topmost powerful governments on the planet. It includes foes and competitors like China and Russia, as well as allies like Germany, France, Great Britain, and Italy. And it is easily one of the largest shifts in financial power and opportunity in the twenty-first century.

The Obama administration had constructed a web of interests involving all the above powers in an entire class of financial interests within the United States. But it had also marginalized many regional countries also traditionally allied to Washington, including the Arab Gulf and Israel. The Iran deal, however, is not representative of diplomacy between countries. It is mostly about gigantic financial interests running from Tehran into the heart of Western Europe, Russia, China, and American powerhouses. In short, what the deal did was obtain a principle from the Islamic Republic of Iran (that it would stop building the nuclear bomb) in return for massive financial interests, starting with the unfreezing of about $150 billion from the West, but that is only the tip of the iceberg.

For the Iranian regime, it was about opening its markets and the markets of the countries it controls—Iraq, Syria, Lebanon, parts of Yemen, and beyond—to international financial groups. What lies beneath is a whole web of American, European, and international interests vying to obtain economic concessions from the Iran regime, creating a two-way bridge of financial interests.

The Obama administration spent six years setting up this super web of cash and financial opportunities. It abandoned four countries entirely—and many other partners—to the Khomeinist regime all for the sake of the deal. A canceling of that hyper-contract is not just about its legacy for the Obama administration. Many commitments by that administration were reversed by the Trump administration, exactly as the Obama White House reversed so many Bush and Reagan achievements. The dismantling of the JCPOA, however, would be worse than losing the election in 2016 with candidate Clinton. It would be the equivalent of removing an entire international system feeding not just one but many governments and financial elites.

Hence, when candidate Trump debuted in 2015 by announcing that he would pull out from the deal and would order his administration to cancel its effects and add sanctions to it, the Obama-Biden administration in its last year was so menaced by this notion that in addition to backing its political heir, presidential candidate Hillary Clinton, it also acted against the Trump campaign, first by launching an intelligence operation to determine how serious the Trump leadership was about taking down the deal if elected, and to discover which foreign policy advisers were involved in talks with Middle Eastern countries that could potentially make this happen. Hence the strange intelligence operation and penetration of a Trump campaign, which was at that point using its positioning regarding the deal more as a foreign policy agenda to attract voters than as an actual policy—which would in fact develop after Trump and his team installed themselves in the White House.

The Obama bureaucracy targeted that Trump campaign,

thinking that an elaborate plan was already at play, and used a Russia canard to discredit, penetrate, and eventually implode a U.S. presidential campaign because of the fear that the latter would eventually become an administration and eliminate the single most important achievement that the Obama White House had left to be protected by its potential successor, a Clinton White House. And after Trump's success in November, the Obama administration moved swiftly to put in place a mechanism that would derail the Trump administration and save the Iran deal in due time.

Obviously, there were many reasons that intersected for the Obama bureaucracy that survived his administration to act against a sitting president and his team, but the Iran deal seems to be the center of the entire resistance against the administration. Some might even propose that the Russia charge was simply a convenient narrative under which the opposition targeted President Trump to prevent his administration, especially General Flynn, who was then the national security adviser, from uncovering the real structure behind the deal. 2017 and most of 2018 were half of a presidential term that became a battleground between a Trump administration trying to survive and reorganize itself while achieving a minimum of goals, including its withdrawal from the Iran deal, and a bureaucratic, political, and media opposition that did everything it could to stop this from happening.

In 2018, Trump still had two majorities in Congress

supporting him months before the House majority would flip to the opposition. The window was quite short, and President Trump pressed on. Obviously what followed was a storm of protests domestically by the opposition shocked by the win, across the pond by Europeans angry about the withdrawal, and east of that by Russia and China shifting their channels to Iran to maintain and increase their dividends from the agreement. But going south to the Middle East, the move was cheered by Israel, applauded by the Arab coalition, and hailed by the Iran opposition and other civil societies and the region. Washington lost the European governments which were profiting from the deal despite the carnage it did in the region, but the partners in the region were joyful that, finally, almost two years after the Riyadh summit, the Trump administration came back to lead after a long fight for its own survival at home.

The withdrawal, which occurred on May 8, 2018, was a strike in the bullseye from the perspective of national security, the war on terror, and pure American national interests. The canceling of U.S. commitment to the JCPOA, even if it was the only achievement by the Trump administration in its first term or only term, was enough to score a vital victory for the West and for the moderates in the Middle East. But after the pullout, the battle of defending that position would last until November 2020.

The pro-Iran deal camp, disoriented by the Trump move, which initially and most likely triggered the opposition's probe and later the impeachment process, escalated its actions domestically and internationally. Once considered only necessary, it was now absolutely vital for the opposition to stop Trump from adding more strikes in the same direction. The remainder of the presidential term would be about blocking Trump politically and trying to remove him via a constitutional process.

Jerusalem

While the world was still digesting Trump's decision to withdraw from the Iran deal, and the opposition was still disoriented by the cataclysmic strike at the JCPOA, one week later, Donald Trump struck again in the Middle East, but this time at the heart of a very old conflict. Risking deterioration of friendly relationships with a number of Arab countries, President Trump opened a U.S. embassy on May 14, 2018, in Jerusalem. This move, promised by several American presidents and many candidates over the previous three decades, was suddenly achieved by a U.S. president under dire attacks by his opposition and parts of his own bureaucracy. Dispatching his daughter Ivanka and son-in-law Jared Kushner and a strong congressional delegation to the opening event in Jerusalem, Trump had one priority: to make sure that his promise of moving the embassy was kept and materialized before his next election—but also before the midterm elections.

Naturally, the Palestinian Authority and a number of Arab governments rejected the decision, and a large cohort of governments across the globe also thought it wasn't the right time, if a good decision at all. But the master of the White House had different calculations and followed a very special strategy. President Trump wanted to secure a U.S. commitment to Israel before he began to bring in the other Arab players—and later the Palestinians. That highly symbolic step on May 14, 2018, would become a stepping-stone for a future move in August 2020 between an important Arab country and Israel.

However, Trump left a stipulation in his speech addressing the issue out of Washington. He noted, in a subtle sentence, that he had moved the U.S. embassy to Jerusalem, but he would be willing to discuss extending Palestinian sovereignty over the Arab neighborhoods of the holy city. He was offering a U.S. recognition of Jerusalem to Israel, bringing back unparalleled support from the Israelis and from many American Jews, but by informing the Palestinians that they would not be marginalized. The Palestinians would launch their administrative capital in a Jerusalem suburb called Abu Dis first, and later as peace takes on a life of its own, he would work with Israelis and Palestinians to attach Arab areas inside Jerusalem to a Palestinian capital. Discretely, a number of Arab governments understood the move and waited for the right time to play their card. The move of the embassy had significant and new repercussions in the U.S. and in Washington in particular.

After having been under stress from prosecutors and the media for more than a year, Donald Trump was making leaps in his initiatives in foreign policy in one of the most difficult and challenging regions of the world. Cancelling the Iran deal and moving the embassy to Jerusalem appealed to a majority of pro-Israel communities at home as these were historic achievements, and hopefully discouraged many from making the irresponsible move of removing the president from the presidency at this critical time when he was defending America from the Iran threat and granting Israel a long-awaited dream. There is little doubt that the Trump camp scored two points against the Obama bureaucracy and may have pushed it to revise its initial plans to use the probe to remove the president from the White House.

Probe Ends

On March 22, 2019, the Mueller probe announced its results and dissolved itself. The probe targeted corruption issues which were mostly sent to the appropriate courts. The report said there were several contacts between members of the campaign and those close to it and several Russian actors and presented evidence. But according to the report, as per Mueller himself, there was no active collaboration between the leadership of the campaign and the Russian leadership, which meant that there was no Trump-Russian conspiracy to defeat the Clinton campaign with Russian participation. That was actually the initial accusation by opposition lawmakers within the House of Representatives in April–May 2017. However, other aspects of the whole laundry list asked by the Republicans close to the Trump administration were not even addressed: the monitoring of the campaign, the unmasking, the FISA Court, and other matters. The back-and-forth between the administration's camp and its opposition in Congress and around Washington would continue regardless until Election Day.

The Mueller probe was the most dangerous phenomenon that had taken place in America since the Civil War. One national party had accused another national party of betraying the country on behalf of another country. Such an accusation is so extreme that, if not proven, it would open a deep wound and revert to counter-accusations from the accused party and from whoever is in charge of the Justice Department. In these matters, if the accuser fails to prove this dramatic accusation, those accused want to know what was behind the accusation, especially if it was a foreign policy issue. The worst outcome would be that the Mueller probe was set up to bring down an American president and his administration in order to stop them from dismantling the policy of a previous administration, a policy that was set up as a joint interest with a foreign government. If indeed the Russia investigation was a mechanism to protect the Iran deal, then it would be tragic for this liberal democracy. The times ahead will tell. Either way, there will be historic consequences.

Designating the IRGC

After the probe was over, the Trump administration had wider space for further action in foreign policy and specifically in the field of national security. It moved forward to complete a policy on Iran after Trump pulled out from the Iran deal in 2018. This first step basically deprived the regime in Tehran from getting income from the deal, receiving frozen Iranian cash. And it also forced companies to choose between doing business with Iran or doing business with the United States. This also deprived the Ayatollahs from making money with non-American entities, putting tremendous strain on Tehran. The latter responded with provocations across the Middle East and against Arab U.S. allies, namely in the Gulf.

The U.S. administration hit on April 8, 2019, with the decision to designate the entire Pasdaran as a terrorist organization, which meant that the nervous center of Iranian politics, economy, and terror activities was slapped with tremendous sanctions, forcing anyone dealing with this organization or with its financial and economic partners to be sanctioned. The bottom line with this decision to designate the Revolutionary Guard as terrorists was that the Trump administration was going all the way to smash the economic and financial ability of the regime to eventually force it to come to the table of negotiations and to bypass the Iran deal and get to a new deal. Obviously, what this meant was that all the brokers and those who were profiting from the initial Iran deal were going to lose their advantages in the next deal. But there may be unintended consequences from a maximum pressure campaign the U.S. started by designating the Pasdaran as a terrorist organization.

Trump was, in fact, also going to war with the regime as a

way to weaken forces profiting from the Iran deal in the first place. The U.S. position was strongly backed by John Bolton, who for years was part of the international opposition coalition against the Iran deal and who wanted something else—a regime change in Iran. In the region, two partners were backing President Trump in his designation of the Pasdaran. First and foremost, Israel was very enthusiastic about this U.S. move and the Israeli prime minister put all her support behind the American decision, calling it also in the vital interest of Israel. In the Arab world, Saudi Arabia, the UAE, and Bahrain were all in full support. Even in Europe, but outside Western Europe, some countries started to side with the Trump administration. Under the coordination of special U.S. envoy Brian Hook, new supporters of the Trump policy emerged, including Poland, Hungary, the Czech Republic, and the Baltics. The newly elected president of Brazil, Jair Bolsonaro, also moved closer to Washington's policy since his leftist predecessors had been hosting Hezbollah and Iran in Brazil for years.

The designation of the IRGC as a terror organization was solidly based on the work of the U.S. intelligence community, including the CIA, DIA, Treasury Department, and other agencies diligently backing the report with evidence and research. The remaining members of the Iran deal, including the Europeans, did not oppose the designation because of the intelligence input. The opposition in Washington had to absorb the move, though some of its members, hardcore apologists for the Iran regime, showed many signs of discomfort with the decision. Politicly, Trump removed a strong player from the chessboard. He was dismantling the strategic partnership established by the Obama administration with the Iran regime and international partners, but he was using objective reasons that all the deal's partners, with the exception of Iran, could not refute or oppose. In the race between the Trump and Obama foreign policies, the opposition lost an important point to the sitting president. Trump survived the Mueller report and hit hard against the Obama Iran policy.

Iran understood Trump shattered Obama's policies. It responded directly and via vassals. On May 12, 2019, UAE ships were sabotaged. On June 12, the Houthis lobbed missiles on the Riyadh airport. Tehran wanted to trigger Washington before it deployed strategic forces in the region. And on June 20, Iranian anti-aircraft missiles downed a U.S. surveillance drone flying in international airspace over the Gulf. Trump ordered a stand-down. He wanted to control the timing of his own actions. Instead, the Pentagon deployed one of the largest deterrents of U.S. forces in the Gulf and later in Iraq and Syria in order to deter Iran. Tehran's calculations were outmaneuvered. The Ayatollahs' goal by conducting several provocations against U.S. allies was fewer American forces in the region. In return, however, Washington put more strategic assets facing Iran across the Gulf and throughout Iraq. Now it was Iran's turn to play. Either it would escalate and risk massive strikes back or it would back off and risk uprisings in the area.

Another Win: Al-Baghdadi Eliminated

On October 19, 2019, President Trump announced that U.S. Special Forces had conducted a raid in northwestern Syria and killed ISIS leader al-Baghdadi. This highly successful yet risky operation was hailed by many in the international community as a symbolic ending of a leadership that was responsible for massacre, ethnic cleansing, and a state of war across the Middle East. The operation was daring as it started in Iraqi Kurdistan and then went into Syrian Kurdistan, penetrating zones in northwestern Syria either under Assad and Russian defense or dominated by jihadist or Muslim Brotherhood militias. This raised President Trump's prestige and credibility, but also raised many questions regarding what was really happening in the region. Al-Baghdadi had taken refuge inside an area controlled by jihadist and Islamist militias, many of whom are connected to Turkey. This again put on the table the whole relationship between the U.S., the Kurds, and Turkey. Along with the operation against Iran's top commander later in January, the Baghdadi elimination unveiled a strategy of eliminating terrorist leaders, something which was also previously adopted by both the Obama and Bush administrations.

CHAPTER 14
APPROACHING CHALLENGES AND MISSED OPPORTUNITIES

My Friend, "Chairman Kim"

2018 was full of surprises launched by Donald Trump as he was maneuvering away from the probe and trying to resolve as many crises and issues as possible. One unexpected surprise was his summit with the leader of North Korea, Chairman Kim Jong Un, in Singapore on June 12, less than a month after the Jerusalem move. The meeting between the two leaders happened in the wake of sudden tremors coming from Kim Jung Un when the North Korean leader ordered the firing of missiles into the Pacific, bypassing the Japanese islands and splashing into the waters of the Pacific. The response by President Trump was different from that of his predecessor.

Chairman Kim, as well as other leaders, had projected that a

U.S. president under siege would refrain from even responding and send secret negotiators to discuss aid and food. But Trump responded differently, first via Twitter, then by dispatching task forces off the Korean Peninsula and mobilizing military assets in Japan. The U.S. president also signaled to Chairman Xi from China that the United States was serious about responding should Kim do anything foolish. The North Korean dictator rushed to Beijing, seeking support, but Xi and the leadership of the Communist Party of China informed him that it was better he negotiate directly with the U.S. and not drag the growing Chinese economy into a unplanned war that would crush the finances of the People's Republic of China.

Communist China of the twenty-first century was different from the one of the fifties and sixties. Its leadership was acting like a business venture capitalist on behalf of the one-party system. Instead of military bases around the world, China developed economic and financial centers and agreements on three continents, Asia, Africa, and North America. Chairman Kim and his regime were still stuck in the ideological framework of the fifties and had not followed China and Vietnam in modernizing their economy. Hunger was widespread, the population was broken, and the cash situation of the country was below zero. They had weapons and a capacity to damage, not the ability to evolve out of the acute crisis.

From the Clinton years through the Obama years, North Korea had one modus operandi. It would threaten the West and the U.S. with military means and obtain aid. Under Trump, things changed. The new equation forced Kim to meet with Trump. Because of the prospect of two controversial leaders appearing together, Trump maneuvered well to get to that meeting with an unpredictable leader in Singapore. The summit by itself obviously did not resolve all the issues, but it froze the prospects of military confrontation. It also encouraged the South Koreans to move forward and meet with Chairman Kim. A greater crisis was avoided during difficult times in Washington, D.C.

The show between Trump and Kim wasn't over. They would meet again on the most publicized spot in the world: the center of the DMZ on the peninsula. The planet would be watching.

Libya

Pursuing a relentless offensive on several foreign policy tracks, Trump surprised the Middle East and Europe one more time when he called Field Marshal Khalifa Haftar, head of the LNA, on April 19, 2019, and discussed "counter-terrorism issues with Haftar." Unexpected, this move disoriented many on all sides of the conflict.

President Trump had moved on Libya, after two years, despite the extreme difficulties facing his own administration regarding the choices to be made in that country at war since 2011. Starting in 2014 the Libyan battlefield can be summarized as follows: In the West of the country, Muslim Brotherhood militias ruled Tripoli, Misurata, and the surrounding areas. They were backed by Qatar and the international Muslim Brotherhood. Later, the AKP government of Erdoğan would join in support of Tripoli. Field Marshal Haftar surged from Benghazi using former soldiers of the regular Libyan army, with which he served in the 1980s, to battle al-Qaeda, ISIS, and eventually the Ikhwan militias between 2014 and 2017. Haftar defeated the jihadists and pushed them out, taking over control of the territories between the Egyptian border and east of Misurata. He was supported by Egypt, the UAE, and, to a lesser extent, France.

The Russians were trying to lure the LNA and its commander to become the main power broker, but Haftar, who had spent twenty years as an exile in Virginia in the United States, was not willing to become another Assad. Rather, he was a nationalist Libyan who wanted to be free from the jihadists and allied to the Arab coalition. He would have been a natural ally of the United States and in the same field as Sisi, MBS, and MBZ.

He was initially appointed as a commander of the armed forces of the only elected body in Libya, the national parliament, which was in exile in Tobruk. In 2015, a UN-sponsored reconciliation conference took place in the city of Skhirat in Morocco and was attended by the parliament, the army, several factions, and the Muslim Brotherhood. It was agreed that an interim government called the GNA would be set up in Tripoli and would be ratified by the elected parliament in Benghazi. The legislative assembly refused to recognize the GNA as long as it was formed and surrounded by Islamist militias. The LNA sided with the elected parliament against the militias. The GNA was fully controlled by the latter. This created the second civil war in Libya between the parliament overseeing the army and the GNA controlled by the Muslim Brotherhood militias.

In Washington, Qatar funded a very powerful lobby to influence the government and all political parties to only recognize the GNA and to lambast the LNA and the parliament. Most of the media followed the Qatari-funded pro-GNA line while just a few lawmakers sided with the LNA. Under the microscope of the war of lobbies, media reports detailed how the Qatar lobby was able to have influence and access on both sides of the divide in Washington, D.C., among the opposition in alliance with the Brotherhood front CAIR, and also within some quarters of the Trump circle. This resulted in a full imbalance in U.S. policy towards Libya. Most of the diplomats in the bureaucracy were citing the so-called UN-recognized government of the GNA. The reality was that the only effectively recognized part of the Morocco agreement was the parliament and the LNA. The Arab coalition felt that President Trump sided with Qatar and the Brotherhood against the parliament and the army, though the Trump line regarding Egypt was that he had sided with the people and the army and not with the Brotherhood, until April 19, when, out of the blue, President Trump and National Security Adviser John Bolton made the phone call to Field Marshal Haftar. It was said that call was made at the request of Egypt's president, Abdel Fattah Sisi, with tacit encouragement from Mohammed bin Salman and Mohammed bin Zayed. From early April, Haftar led an offensive that took his troops very close to Tripoli from the south. Many observers thought that he got a green light from President Trump.

Venezuela

Leaping from Libya, the Trump administration moved on Venezuela immediately. On April 30, 2019, Bolton said "all options are on the table regarding the ongoing protests."

The situation in Venezuela had developed more dramatically than before. The Maduro regime engaged in suppression of the mass demonstrations. Pompeo and Bolton lent support to the demonstrators and eventually led an international campaign to recognize the head of the elected parliament, which was controlled by the opposition, hoping for the formation of an alternative government headed by Juan Guaidó. The Trump administration was moving fast to regain time and push back against rogue regimes allied to Iran. The Guaidó government was recognized by the Organization of American States (OAS), the European Union, and Canada, which amounted to a major success for the White House. However, the president did not estimate that taking direct action in Venezuela was timely while his national security adviser, Bolton, disagreed. It was clear that Trump was gaining back what he lost the first two years because of the probe. But beyond the new U.S. policy towards Venezuela, it was also Iran's influence in that country that was put under pressure by the U.S.

China Talks

Since day one in office, President Trump was thinking about what moves to take to engage Chairman Xi of China to resolve American problems with the country. The first move was to remove the United States' economic stress due to its debt to China. The second was to cut a new deal with Beijing based on a more balanced economic and financial relationship. Donald Trump as an international businessman was familiar with and had deep knowledge about Chinese-American financial relationships. He was ready to take on this problem, notwithstanding that it became a systemic one. The mirror amount of debts owed by the U.S. to China was by itself a near impossible mission to resolve in just a few years, let alone while the United States was involved in many conflicts, sending foreign aid to scores of countries, and committed to fund many international organizations and projects. The Chinese economic machine was conquering markets around the world, particularly in Asia, Africa, and Latin America. Since the country was admitted to the World Trade Organization during the 1990s and American interests moved to China en masse because of cheap labor, the Communist Party of China was acting like an uber capitalist enterprise while maintaining control through the Communist Party on the political level.

Presumably, President Trump wanted to achieve the goal of a China-U.S. economic agreement in the first year of his presidency in response to a commitment to winning his 2016 campaign where he heavily criticized China and the Obama administration for allowing Beijing to profit immensely from the U.S. economy and in return not helping America get out of the financial trap it was driven to. But the effects of the probe against the White House were also felt on that sensitive front. No major deal was possible between Trump and Xi before the end of the probe, which would have allowed a more comfortable situation for White House teams to prepare for a resolution of the bilateral problems before the end of 2019.

Meeting on the DMZ

On June 30, 2019, Donald Trump met with Chairman Kim at the limit of the DMZ between South and North Korea. In a scene from a movie adapted from the Cold War, President Trump crossed the line with the North Korean leader, walked for a few feet, took pictures, and made a statement before walking back to South Korea.

The moment was presented as a chance for peace and a possible deal between the United States and the North Korean Communist regime. However, it was known in the circle of experts that despite the awful photo op, the treaty to resolve the nuclear challenge on the peninsula had to be approved by China. Nevertheless, the explosive East Asia situation was treated with morphine. Chairman Kim was satisfied to be elevated to the rank of international leader instead of a rogue leader like Assad and Maduro. But he was far from letting his missile and nuclear weapon system go before ensuring the safety of his regime.

President Trump was satisfied that he could use a stunt to maintain that stable front for the time being.

Missed Opportunity: The Second Middle East Revolution

As President Trump entered the realm of this second massive investigation of his presidential term, the impeachment inquiry, a massive second revolution exploded in the heart of the Middle East. Starting in Baghdad in early October, demonstrations spread out in the city against oppression by the Iran-backed militias, known as popular mobilization units or, in Arabic, *Hashd Shaabi*. The protests widened and people demanded the resignation of the Iran-backed government amidst full paralysis in most of the country.

On October 17, 2019, a huge protest also exploded in downtown Beirut, targeting the Hezbollah-controlled government and demanding resignation of the president, the cabinet, and the speaker of the parliament. Revolution quickly spread to multiple cities, including to Tripoli in the north, Sidon in the south, and stunningly and for the first time into areas traditionally controlled by Hezbollah in the south of Lebanon and in the Bekaa Valley. The Beirut uprising was the second revolution in Lebanon since the Cedar Revolution in March 2014. But this Lebanese revolt was wider, stronger, and sustained for months. It was reported that close to two million people had at one time or another participated in the autumn revolt across Lebanon. Soon enough, towards the end of the month, protests erupted across Iran from the capital to several other cities and provinces.

The third country to catch fire by protests was Iran itself, when tens of thousands of Iranians from all backgrounds took to the streets against the regime.

The revolution in the Middle East was catching fire. But in all three countries, suppression was the systematic answer. The Iran regime, which coordinated the strategic activities of all four regimes, including in Syria, could not afford retreating, accepting resignations, or engaging in deep reforms. Any weakening anywhere from Tehran to Beirut would lead to the collapse of all four regimes just as it happened between 1989 in 1991 in Eastern Europe and the Soviet Union.

In Iraq, the masses of demonstrators showed huge numbers, mostly of young protesters, a clear majority of them from Shia neighborhoods in Baghdad and throughout the south. It was in fact an uprising by Shia Arabs against the Iranian regime occupation. Other communities in Iraq were also represented well in the daily clashes between protesters and security forces backed by the violent, armed pro-Iran militias. Many people have been killed; thousands have been wounded; hundreds have been detained. The revolution in all three countries was genuine and, most importantly, not supported by foreign governments. In fact, men and women on social media and, when they could appear, on Arab and Middle Eastern TV have called on the U.S. government and specifically President Trump to intervene and stop the bloodshed against the population. The moment was ripe for a historic change to take place in the Middle East by non-lethal means. But the regimes under the control of the Ayatollahs would not accept a peaceful transfer of power. The demonstrators then turned to the international community and to the United States.

Here again the Trump administration faced a major dilemma. These were historic opportunities like the ones of Eastern Europe in 1989, where the people could rise to end the totalitarian regimes, form other governments against the terrorist networks, counter extremist ideologies, and on their own, defend their countries with support from the United States and other willing partners. The opportunity was indeed enormous, but once again the planets were not aligned.

The Trump administration was pounded by the congressional majority, media, and outside bodies like the Iran regime and others who saw an opportunity for Trump to be taken out of the picture as these revolts were taking place. The removal of the Iran deal incurred a tremendous cost, both to the regime and to its partners worldwide—and probably even within the United States. Designation of the IRGC added losses to the Iran regime. And as of October, the entire Iran axis was shaking as a result of the revolutions. But just at that moment when the Khomeinist empire was at its weakest in decades, suddenly the pro-Iran deal core within the U.S. opposition launched a mega investigation aimed at impeaching the leader of the free world, practically stopping him from reaching out to the populations revolting against the pro-

Iranian regimes in the region. The coincidence was once again too neat.

The probe of 2017 came just before President Trump traveled to Riyadh to form an Arab coalition, and also before his national security team could craft a strategy to reverse the Iran deal. Now, during the fall of 2019, as the revolutions in the Middle East were threatening to bring down the Iranian regime and its satellites, another investigation was launched from the same quarters that organized the 2017 probe.

The revolutions were sustained for more than three months through the end of the year and into a few weeks of 2020, until suppression and the coronavirus spread, bringing them to a halt.

Secretary Pompeo issued several tweets in support of the three revolutions in the Middle East, and President Trump issued a couple tweets himself to salute the protesters. But the administration was not ready to engage in full support for several reasons. First, as indicated, the impeachment dragged the White House into a focused defense against the charges. Second, any engagement with the three revolutions would have needed wider logistical supplies and spending to sustain U.S. support as well as probably a military region deployment in support of such policy. Congress would have opposed it very sharply. The pro-Iran deal majority in the House would never have openly supported a revolt against the very regime it wanted to re-engage to revive the Iran deal. Last but not least, frankly, the Trump administration did not have the right strategy or team, at that point, to wage a campaign in a war of ideas. Hence, the huge opportunity the revolutions represented was missed, at least for the time being. The civil societies in the region were depressed, but they never knew that the partners of the Iran deal inside the United States were the actual reason why their revolutions were not supported by the United States at that point in time. It would take a second Trump administration to refuel the Middle Eastern revolts; otherwise, should the opposing camp win, the anti-Iran regime revolution would be lost for another generation.

Turkey Prepares for Libya

Just before the end of 2019, other storms were brewing, taking advantage of the Washington infighting over impeachment. Among them, the AKP government of Mr. Erdoğan was feverishly preparing for a military campaign in Libya. By December 5, the Turkish Parliament authorized a military expedition into western Libya to support the GNA government and the Brotherhood ministers against the LNA and Libyan Parliament. This was stunning as Mr. Erdoğan knew that President Trump had phoned Field Marshal Haftar. Why would Ankara invade Libya and fight the LNA knowing that a U.S. president called to congratulate this army for its work against the jihadists? Probably because the Muslim Brotherhood and Qatar were informed by the opposition that the Trump administration was pinned down by the impeachment and would thus be unable to react to the Libyan situation. And that is practically what happened.

CHAPTER 15

2020: THE YEAR OF CORONA AND RIOTS

The last year of Donald Trump's term witnessed the highest levels of social incidents and political warfare inside the country while around the world, conflicts reached a point of boiling with no sense of stabilization. In Washington, the supporters of the old Obama agenda were getting ready to launch a campaign to elevate his former vice president, Joe Biden, as the next presidential candidate on behalf of the opposition. President Donald Trump would endure the impeachment battle, coordinate the coronavirus response, withstand the U.S. riots in the summer, sponsor two Israel peace accords with the UAE and Bahrain, and relentlessly engage in the presidential campaign leading up to November 3. He led amidst a rough environment and remained committed to his foreign policy despite the harsh resistance by the proponents of an Obama-Biden reversal policy all the way through the elections.

The Soleimani War

As the three revolutions in Iran, Iraq, and Lebanon persisted throughout December, Iran-backed militias in Baghdad and across the country started striking at U.S. forces deployed in some regions and targeted the U.S. embassy. The U.S. government warned these militias that American forces would defend themselves and strike back. Somehow the leaders of the militia, probably badly advised, believed that the Trump administration was completely overwhelmed by the domestic crisis, including the impeachment process, and was thus very weak and would be less likely to respond militarily to any moves against the U.S. military.

Events on the ground changed rapidly as the various Iraqi militias backed by the Quds force moved constantly to harass and target U.S. positions. The U.S. embassy was surrounded by militiamen who tried to set it ablaze. A chain reaction of incidents led to a confrontation in Kirkuk leaving an American contractor dead. President Trump gave the order to strike back against the highest level of the militia network, regardless of the impeachment since the White House considered attacks against U.S. troops as a matter of national security that needed to be addressed immediately. On January 3, 2020, a strike by the U.S. military took out the Quds Force commander, Qassem Soleimani, along with Iraq militia commanders near the Baghdad airport. The strike sent shockwaves across Iraq and the Middle East, drawing a thick red line around U.S. forces operating in the region. The

Iranian leadership had misread the decision by President Trump the previous year to not respond to the downing of the U.S. drone flying over the Gulf. But in this cycle of clashes in early January, Iran-backed Iraqi forces closed in on two American bases and crossed the red line. The U.S. response surprised the Ayatollahs and the Pasdaran. It sent a strong message to our foes (and friends) in the region that despite the severity of the internal political situation in Washington, Trump would strike back at Iranian assaults and violence.

However, the most surprising element to come out regarding the U.S. strike on the top commander of all Iranian militias and the Middle East was coordinated attacks on Trump, the White House, and his administration for actually striking back at Iranian assets who were planning a series of attacks against U.S. targets. Members of the U.S. House, think tanks, and media talking heads assaulted Trump for ordering such an attack on what they called a high-level official in the Iranian Armed Forces! The criticism amounted more to a panic among the supporters of the Iran deal than an objective evaluation of who Soleimani was and the atrocities he was responsible for. The opposition was concerned that the escalation in Iraq with Iran by the Trump administration would damage the ability of the opposition to come back to the deal and revive it.

The Coronavirus Pandemic

In the early days of January 2020, the first videos appeared on YouTube about men and women in China, more specifically in the Wuhan province, getting sick, falling on the ground, and then being hospitalized. This was the beginning of the pandemic that would reach the four corners of the world and strike at world health and economy. The novel coronavirus, known later as COVID-19, was born in the district of Wuhan and from there infected the whole world. But that January of 2020, the majority in the U.S. House of Representatives was busy and focused on organizing the impeachment process of President Donald Trump.

The very first step taken by the administration in response to the virus was to ban all flights coming from China, where COVID-19 originated. At the time, the opposition media pounded the White House for even raising the issue of the coronavirus threat, accusing the president of diverting attention from what it considered the most important priority: impeaching the president himself. Accusations of racism and xenophobia during the impeachment quickly turned to accusations that Trump did not do enough early enough to develop a strategy to contain and stop the spread of the virus.

Then the Trump administration's withdrawal from the World Health Organization drew criticism from the opposition on the grounds of the principle. But the reality was that the organization did not quickly react to the problem inside China—and did not inform the rest of the world in the most urgent manner. Washington believes that the WHO is politically closer to China and was thus attempting to dodge any criticism of, for, or from

Beijing. The opposition in the U.S. slammed Trump's decision to pull out from the organization, but in view of the devastation that the virus has caused to America, it seems there may actually be a need for fundamental reform inside the WHO before resuming normal relations between the U.S. and the organization.

The U.S. Riots and Homeland Security

On May 25, 2020, an African American citizen was killed during an arrest by police officers in Minneapolis. George Floyd's death sparked riots in the city, then across the country, with demonstrations reaching the major urban centers of the United States, including Washington, D.C. The larger peaceful protests expressed anger and frustration within communities and a segment of society regarding police violence and lack of training among some law enforcement crews. The outcry was just and resonated nationwide. However, a radical stream of the movement jumped on the incident and took it in a far different direction. That street injustice in Minneapolis, like many similar incidents before throughout the nation, was to be addressed and resolved firmly by the U.S. justice system, but other forces at play whisked it from the court system and hijacked it to the realm of organized urban violence, in an ideological framework seeking regime change in America.

Two radical forces dove into the protests and tried to divert them towards violence, first by burning and destroying public and private property, destroying police precincts, then attacking individual citizens and police officers. The violent riots, organized by a network able to move militants within a city and across the country, escalated their narrative and their action rapidly. First, the radicals demanded the removal of security from all areas of rioting. Then they moved to demands for dismantling and/or defunding police departments.

Two major movements led the riot campaign across the country. One was the movement Antifa, and the other was Black Lives Matter. The first group launched in America in the mid-1990s and is an amalgam of neo-Bolshevik and anarchist groups seeking the collapse of what they describe as the "capitalist state" to instead erect the ultimate "regime of the people," which in practice would be a Stalinist-type government. In parallel, another neo-Marxist movement, self-styled as Black Lives Matter, started as a protest group against police excesses in African American neighborhoods. While the stated goal of BLM was legitimate and inspiring within the community and across the country, to enhance social peace and equality, the Far Left component of the group was pushing more of an extremist ideology which sought the delegitimization of America as a country and to replace it with a radical regime. Both Antifa and BLM followed the same tactic: professing to seek a more just society while in fact promoting extreme mass violence, cultural and ethnic divisions, and undermining national unity.

Soon enough, the militants of the radical movement started attacking statues representing the Founding Fathers of America, way beyond protesting and asking for the removal of military commanders of the South during the American Civil War. The radicalized part of the riots was no longer part of the general protest to stop police brutality tactics, but morphed into a fully-fledged "anti-American" message aimed at the dismantlement of the foundations and the democratic structures of the United States while shielding itself with the narrative of victimhood and civil strife among communities. The radicals move to reject the American flag, the United States Constitution, and American institutions, working to rewrite American history in a fashion to adhere to their ideology—as all totalitarian movements have tried to impose, from the Bolsheviks in Russia to the national socialists of Germany to the Khomeinists in Iran to the jihadists across the Middle East and beyond. The urban radicals in America seem to want to repeat the Bolshevik experience of 1917 and the Khomeini experience of 1979. But in the age of social media and free thinking, civil societies reject these experiences which have always led to tragedies, wars, famines, massive breaches of human rights, and other disasters.

The American radicals seem to be the product of a deep failure in the U.S. educational system, which has been under the control of radicals from all ideologies brainwashing in the classrooms for decades. The American constitutional system and traditions give freedom of speech to all Americans, moderates and extremists alike. However, some among the extremists use American freedoms to destroy the system that protects these freedoms. This is the fine but dangerous line between political protests and a violent takeover of a democratic republic. The nature of the American public as tested before will not accept the diktat of fringe radicals. America is too large and Americans too free to submit to totalitarians. The only results that the latter could achieve using and abusing the freedom protected by the Constitution are chaos, violence, economic setback, and election mayhem.

There is certainly a difference between peaceful protesters and reformers on the one hand and violent riots and radicals on the other hand. Usually, the political establishment comes together to support the reformers and isolate the violent extremists. However, in 2020 it was different. While the Trump administration, expressing the feelings and the will of the silent majority, fearing the violent upheaval and the calls to disband the police, moved in the right sense of history to protect citizens and communities and back up the police, the opposition leadership, surprisingly to many, openly supported the rioters, calling them peaceful demonstrators.

This is important to note because it is evident of the radicalization of the Obama and now Biden platform as they agree with most of what the radicals were calling for, threatening civilians who do not submit to such ideas as eliminating the police, which would lead to instant chaos, paralyzing the institutions until the administration agrees to abide by their agenda or quit their positions.

Such support of the violent extremists from the leaders of the previous administration, when added to the action taken by their supporters in the bureaucracies to remove Trump and his associates from government, demonstrates that the opposition leadership, the media, and the rioters were and are all in one camp with one goal, regime change in America.

Another troubling dimension to the radical riots were the calls for support that came from the radicals overseas, including in the Middle East, as Iranian regime supporters, Hezbollah, Hamas, the Muslim Brotherhood, the Maduro regime, Castrists, and other radicals around the world openly supported the rioters and in many places called them the *intifada* of America.

Here again, most Americans should be able to see that the choices have become narrower and narrower when it comes to the safety of citizens and the national security of the country. The violent rioters are backed politically by the leadership of the opposition and supported overseas by the vast network of regimes and organizations who are enemies of the United States.

Foreign Hot Spots

The politically motivated impeachment trial of Donald Trump ended on February 5 with an acquittal from the U.S. Senate—an acquittal that was never in doubt because the process was never about a conversation with the president of Ukraine, no matter how hard the opposition and media tried to make it look that way. As the opposition in the U.S. Congress sought to further delegitimize the presidency, this encouraged various foreign actors to upset the balance of power in more than one spot around the world, and another military development soon occurred when Turkey decided to invade western Libya, sending troops, armored drones, missiles, and other equipment. Turkey's goal is to defend the GNA government and the Islamist militias, defeat the LNA, and conquer a large swath of land in the western provinces of Libya.

The Beirut Explosion

On August 4, 2020, a cataclysmic explosion in Beirut destroyed the entire port and with it a third of the city. Hundreds were killed, thousands were wounded, and the capital was in shambles. The drama unveiled the dark reality of Lebanon: Hezbollah controls the entire country, from its government to its strategic positions. This was a rude awakening for the majority of Lebanese who seek freedom and a normal life. The explosion was cataloged as possibly the third most powerful explosion since 1945. It looked like a nuclear mushroom and spread fear in the hearts of the population, which spread to the entire world via TV. This was one of the indirect effects of the Iran deal designed by the Obama/Biden administration in coordination with the Ayatollahs. The U.S. under the previous administration sent $150 billion to the Islamic Republic of Iran, which in turn sent loads of cash money to its vessel in Lebanon, Hezbollah, which also in turn spent it to further control the small country, including building a base of operations inside the port of Beirut, where it was said that

Hezbollah owned and managed huge warehouses as weapon depots and dangerous materiel storage.

The tragic explosion opened the file of Iran control of Lebanon, in parallel to Iraq, Syria, and Yemen. Many have asked what the Trump administration could have done to change the reality. Washington has worked tirelessly over the past three years to put sanctions on Hezbollah and its allies, but to go beyond the sanctions into more active measures, the administration needed to have enough space and support to build a resistance against Hezbollah. And that is precisely what the House opposition rejected under the aegis of a bill limiting the president's ability to conduct operations that was passed by the Democrat majority. Furthermore, the Inquisition type of probe imposed on the administration for three and a half years paralyzed the ability of U.S. foreign policy to help the Lebanese people rise against Hezbollah—as was also the case in Iraq, *and* in Venezuela. The Beirut explosion, like many other tragedies in the Middle East, was the result of a strategically dangerous deal made with a strategically dangerous regime—initiated by the Obama administration. The people in the Middle East, and an increasing majority in the United States, have been conscious that a new U.S. policy in the Middle East needs to be shaped.

The UAE-Bahrain-Israel Abraham Accord

On August 13, 2020, President Donald Trump announced that the UAE and Israel decided to sign a peace agreement between themselves with the sponsorship of the United States. Israel agreed to freeze some West Bank land nationalization, and the Emirates agreed to fully normalize with Israel—and both countries would exchange embassies. A few weeks later Bahrain followed suit. Many around the world were surprised; a few were not. I was among those few because I witnessed the genesis and evolution of that dialogue between the three countries. The Trump administration obviously scored a major diplomatic victory, which could become even wider if Trump is re-elected in November 2020. Other Arab countries, particularly Saudi Arabia, Sudan, Morocco, and Oman, joining the agreement would change the political and strategic landscape of the Middle East. It has been over twenty-five years since Israel has entered into a peace agreement with another Arab country. In 1994, it was Jordan. And before that, in 1979, it was the Camp David Accords with Egypt. Throughout the intervening years, Israel has been ready to enter into a peace agreement with any willing Arab country, but the radical forces in the Middle East have blocked such an agreement for decades. The Iran regime and the Muslim Brotherhood have opposed any peace agreement between Israel and any Arab country with all means possible.

Hamas, an ally of Iran and recipient of their help, and Hezbollah in Lebanon, as well as all Jihadist forces in the region, have kept the Middle East on fire, blocking any attempt to conclude peace between the Jewish state and other Arab countries. When the UAE and Bahrain opportunities came, the Israelis rushed toward them and sought the help of the Trump White

House to guarantee the process. The leaders of the UAE under Sheikh Mohammed bin Zayed have been preparing for a massive cultural and ideological change within their federation of principalities for decades. Abu Dhabi was one of the first Arab capitals to set up the longest list of terrorist and extremist organizations in the Arab world. Cutting a deal with the United States and Israel over a peace agreement was part of a much more comprehensive plan to mitigate new geopolitical realities with three goals: (1) to contain Iran, (2) to fight Islamist extremism, and (3) to move towards accelerated modernization. The accord between the two countries signaled that all three goals could be achieved and was thus applauded by many in the Arab world in the Middle East and around the world. President Trump became the architect of this new twist in regional history.

President Trump was nominated by a conservative European politician as a potential candidate for the Nobel Peace Prize for his sponsorship of the Abraham agreement. All leaders who make peace possible should deserve such recognition, including Arabs and Israelis, and in particular in the 2020 cycle, Mohammed bin Zayed, who inspired the renewal of the peace agreements after decades of stagnation.

Divergent Messages from the Two National Conventions

The conventions held by the two major parties in August 2020 sent two starkly different messages to the American folders and public. The Democratic National Convention held from August 17 through the 20 told the American people that the once left-of-center Democratic body has shifted towards its Far Left, changing the landscape of American politics, similar to what has happened in other democracies, including France, Germany, Italy, and Israel. The traditional Left of liberal and social Democrats has vanished and has been replaced by a more authoritarian, intolerant, and insecure Left, lost between neo-Marxism and anti-liberalism. On foreign policy the Democratic convention committed to a return to the Iran deal, an alliance with the Muslim Brotherhood, and a partnership with Far Left movements across the world. The party of John F. Kennedy, Martin Luther King, Jr., Tom Lantos, and Joe Lieberman has dissipated. The Obama-Biden vision for foreign policy and national security, which included support to radicals overseas and standing by radicals at home, was reinforced in their message.

The Republican National Convention, in contrast and in reaction to the radicalization of the other party, held on and shifted further toward a patriotic conservative line. It committed to the full dismantling of the Iran deal, and a decisive defeat of the jihadists while also rejecting the radical agenda both at home and overseas.

The Biden-Harris contrast with the Trump-Pence agenda was like night and day. The American public was offered a choice on domestic, economic, social, and political levels that could not be clearer, and an even starker choice in foreign affairs and national security. The choice for Americans on November 3, 2020, should be inspired from the two directions that have never been as distinct as they were during the summer of 2020. The choice actually made on Election Day will impact public life in the United States and the destiny of America for years to come.

CHAPTER 16
2020 REEMERGENCE
OR GOING BACKWARD

Trump emerged from the impeachment politically wounded and bleeding but still moving forward and scoring foreign policy points despite the tidal wave of attacks by the combined forces of the Democrat opposition, the media, the lobbies, and even a small elite segment from the Republican Party. On all overseas files the White House maintained the line and further developed positive policies and agendas when possible. It would have been difficult for any U.S. president to continue to press forward in foreign policy while being systematically attacked by an impressive assortment of political forces in the domestic arena, but the Iran deal was still dead in America and more sanctions were leveled against the regime in Iran, the militias in Iraq, the Assad clan in Syria, Hezbollah in Lebanon, and even the Houthis in Yemen. The probe and the impeachment bled the president individually but did not defeat his policy. It was slowed down but continued to move forward.

However, on another front, the Muslim Brotherhood lobbies were more capable in scoring points in Washington while the White House was engaging in fighting the battle of the Iran deal worldwide and at home. And the reason why the Ikhwan was more capable in scoring victories in Libya, Syria, Yemen, and beyond was the powerful lobby they built in the United States. But the Trump base is deeply opposed to the Islamist ideology and movement. Hence, despite their influence, the Brotherhood fronts won't exert more impact on the administration in the long run, if Trump wins the election. But if Trump does not win, they will expand quite widely.

The Counter-Investigation

After the probe was over in 2019, the Justice Department opened an investigation of the probe itself and sought to determine whether the individuals or agencies that were involved in monitoring the Trump campaign in 2016—as well as his administration in 2017—did anything wrong or illegal. The counter-investigation was assigned to John Durham, an attorney general in Connecticut. Apart from the strict legal and criminal part of the investigation, many questions rose into the realm of counterintelligence and of foreign influence.

The Obama administration, which ordered the initial investigation, spying and harvesting information about those in the Trump orbit, raises many questions. Why was Donald Trump put under this type of inquiry and why were his associates pursued and then surely harassed? Was it a legitimate law enforcement operation? No investigations of Trump or his personnel, whether the congressional inquiry or the Mueller probe, found any legal wrongdoing regarding foreign intervention by the Trump campaign or presidency. Was it purely power politics, a simple attempt to remove a president and replace him with another?

This would be quite stunning for a true democratic republic like the United States. Because America allows elections cyclically, there was no need to remove a president before his term ended unless his actions were damaging something very important, if not vital, for the interests of his opposition. Historians may someday clear this up, but in my view, this all looks like it was an extreme opposition designed to paralyze the administration and eventually stop it from pursuing its various policies, specifically U.S. foreign policy.

Using the powerful agencies of government to change the policies of an administration against the will of its top elected official, the president, is destructive to the national accord of the country. But doing so to satisfy foreign interests as well is destructive to the national security of the country.

CONCLUSION

WHAT IS AWAITING
AMERICA IN THE WORLD

As Americans navigate through the 2020 elections, emerging or renewed leadership in November 2020 will have to address the state of the country's national security. Since the end of World War II, throughout the Cold War, and in the years following 9/11, the American nation never stopped holding the burden of sacrifices, in blood and treasure, in defense of liberty worldwide, and freedom at home. But present times and the near future are presenting this country with the greatest dangers since the Civil War. America is facing tremendous and historic choices regarding how it will handle global threats overseas and in the homeland.

Washington in the next months and years will certainly still be facing off with geopolitical and economic competitors who sometimes turn into foes but not necessarily warring parties. Russia and China are the main members of that circle. The U.S.

will need to deal with them in many sectors, from the UN Security Council and international security issues to world economy and energy matters to trade. But at the same time, these frenemies are involved with real enemies of the United States, who supply them, protect them, shield them from sanctions, and at times use them to block American agendas around the world. The next leadership in the White House should be able to sustain an intelligent, comprehensive, and global state of engagement and containment regarding these superpowers.

Which foreign policy would most Americans trust to deal with the relationship with these great powers? The Obama school type of policy where he was emboldened to say to the Russian leadership he would have more flexibility, as was the case when the former president asked President Medvedev in 2012 to be patient with him because he had a last election? The policy that we saw starting in 2013 whereby Washington at the time was unable to block Russia and China from arming Iran? A policy that allowed Iran to obtain $150 billion and then use that cash to buy weapons from both Russia and eventually China?

Or a policy with the strength needed to exert pressure on such foreign governments to adhere to policy designed by the United States, and pressure them to get the right agreements on security and/or on economy, as was the case with the Trump administration? When Donald Trump wanted to message a vassal of Russia, he had no issue targeting weapons of mass destruction on a Syrian base with the Russian military around. And at the same time, when it was needed, his administration's military commands coordinated with the Russian forces on the ground in Syria to ensure that ISIS and the jihadists were destroyed and the Kurds protected. As for China, despite the fact that Trump openly and quickly focused on the American interests in the Chinese economy, he was also able to reach a peer-to-peer deal regarding the Paris treaty and other trade issues in early 2020. With great, powerful but somewhat competitive foes in a time of hostile powers, the Reagan-Trump approach may work better.

Which foreign policy is best for America when it has to do with rogue, radical, and terrorist regimes and organizations, like the Khomeinist regime, its allies in Iraq, Syria, Lebanon, and Yemen, or the Taliban, ISIS, al-Qaeda, and jihadi militias around the world? The Obama-Biden policies that empowered the Iran regime with a dizzying amount of cash used for the purchase of advanced weapons and to enable terrorist organizations across the Middle East in Iraq, Lebanon, and Yemen? An Iran deal that delayed freedom among Iranians, Iraqis, Syrians, Lebanese, and others—and was even used to buy influence on multiple continents? And the Iran deal which most likely was the reason for which bureaucracies in Washington and other Western capitals exerted influence on their own foreign policy? The type of foreign policy that, in the United States, encouraged these bureaucracies to stage a coordinated campaign to bring down a presidency just so that the deal is preserved?

In contrast, the Trump administration opposed the

catastrophic Iran deal, maintained that policy despite all the political pressure produced by the Iran lobby within the United States, was immune to propaganda blasts, withdrew from the deal as soon as it could, deployed all the assets in the Middle East needed to contain the Iranian terror expansion, built an international alliance, and maintained a single consistent message for four years.

With or against the Iran deal is the central parameter against which to compare and contrast Obama and Trump foreign policies. One administration was in power for eight years and took an incalculable and dangerous risk by empowering a very dangerous terror regime. The other administration took all imaginable political risk to satisfy a national security priority in its four years.

On counterterrorism, we see another major contrast between the two doctrines. The Obama administration partnered with the Islamists during the Arab Spring, allowing civil societies to be overrun by jihadists. And worst of all, it partnered with a radical dangerous network which not only was part of an Islamist takeover in the Greater Middle East, but also has been and continues to be behind one of the two most formidable indoctrination and radicalization machines on the planet. Versus the Trump administration that announced, at least in public, that it would oppose jihadism, engage effectively against indoctrination, and coordinate with Arab and Muslim countries in their efforts against extremism. Between the two agendas, the difference is night and day.

The last four years are in stark contrast with the policy of the previous eight years under Obama. In the Trump administration, one can find weaknesses, shortcomings, wrong appointments in the executive teams, half-implemented policies, wrong advice to the president, and more, but one overarching and vital characteristic is that President Trump, for the past four years, has been going in the right strategic direction. *That* is the major difference between Trump and Obama.

The Choice: Biden or Trump

So despite the charges of Islamophobia and racism, all the media attacks, the spying on the campaign, the Russia investigation and Mueller probe, the early firing of essential personnel, the Kirkuk crisis, the Venezuela crisis, Chinese expansion and trade imbalance, losing the House to the opposition in midterm elections, an unjustified impeachment trial, the COVID-19 pandemic, and urban uprisings around the country...Trump was able to pass tax reform, create an Arab coalition, withdraw from the Iran deal, defeat ISIS, recognize Jerusalem as the capital of Israel and move the U.S. embassy there while not marginalizing the Palestinians, have not one but two historic meetings with North Korea's Chairman Kim, get the border crisis under control, eliminate Soleimani, get the IRGC back on the terrorist list, broker a peace deal between Israel, the UAE, and Bahrain, and reverse Obama's foreign policy that gave extremists influence in our own government, illegally and unconstitutionally targeted a political opposition, and had little to do with national security. Obviously, no administration is ever completely error- or problem-free, and the Trump administration is no exception, but the alternative option, a Biden administration, would bring about significant strategic mistakes in national security and foreign policy.

But even though the media does a pretty good job of keeping Americans focused on domestic issues like the economy, law and order within our cities, infighting among states, and division in the populace based on background, culture, and status, if it were to take a good look at what is actually in the best interests of the United States of America and its own safety, it should look to the differences in foreign policy agendas.

Times have changed. We truly are a geopolitical world. Americans need to wake up and decide what they want—liberty, prosperity, security, friendly alliances, and rule of law at home and around the world—or Islamist influence, a nuclear Iran and North Korea, constitutional melting, and political corruption, including the fact the U.S. government will now constitute an elite that will always be above the law, and foreign relations that do not put the interests of Americans first, but instead work to increase and maintain power.

That is what is at stake in foreign policy and national security—condition sine qua non to defend our very identity.

EPILOGUE

After reading this essay, I believe citizens should realize the appropriate direction for U.S. foreign policy and which choice should be made in 2020 and in the years to come. On November 3, the American people will make a choice, which I hope will be the most informed possible. Because what is at stake is the very national security of the United States. In view of the menaces accumulating overseas, from Iran to Hezbollah, ISIS, al-Qaeda, global and local jihadists, dangerously armed dictatorships like North Korea and Venezuela, and the nefarious activities coming from the two major geopolitical foes Russia and China, and of the violent factions conducting urban upheaval within the United States, it is crucial that Americans see the options they have, understand them, and make a decisive choice in these troubling times to attain a peace and stability overseas—and security, safety, and prosperity at home.

The choice this year in 2020 is between President Donald Trump and the new administration he would form in 2021 to respond to the national security challenges, and former vice president Joe Biden, who would form an administration reflecting a third term of former president Obama's direction.

American citizens will create the future that they now choose.

ACKNOWLEDGMENTS

There are so many persons I would like to thank since I published my last book in 2014. In those six years, I've received support in my research and daily commentary from community leaders, producers, analysts, and of course my family. They were standing by my side the whole time, especially during the rough years 2016-2017, which inspired my decision to write this book.

My special thanks go to my agent Lynne Rabinoff, my senior editor Dorothy Logan, and my "special analyst," as well as to my several dedicated and loyal assistants over the past half-decade, including Rebecca Bynum and Sumner Park.

Special thanks to the publisher, Post Hill Press, and all those that helped to get this book to market at this time.

This book is dedicated to my faithful readers, fans, friends, and those patriot Americans who are concerned about the present and future of our country, The United States of America.

And in remembrance of my late father Halim, my mother Hind, and other loved ones who have passed to the next world.

A testimony for truth, a hope for justice, and a search for real peace.

ABOUT THE AUTHOR

Dr. Walid Phares was a foreign policy advisor to U.S. presidential candidate Donald Trump in 2016 and a national security advisor to U.S. presidential candidate Mitt Romney in 2012. He has been a Middle East and Terrorism analyst at Fox News since 2007 and is presently a national security and foreign policy analyst with Fox News and Fox Business channel. He often appears on other American and international media. Phares has advised members of the U.S. Congress and the European Parliament and has been co-secretary general of the Transatlantic Parliamentary Group since 2008.

Phares is the author of fourteen books in English, French, and Arabic, including *Future Jihad*, which made it on the Foreign Policy bestseller list, as well as the prescient *The Coming Revolution* and *The Lost Spring*. He briefs national security and intelligence agencies, advises NGOs and INGOs, and has taught at various universities. He has served as a defense lawyer, translator, journalist, and expert witness in political asylum cases since 1981.

Born in Beirut, Lebanon, Walid Phares immigrated to the United States in 1990.

For more information about the author and his work visit www.walidphares.com or find him on Twitter @walidphares.

Made in the USA
Coppell, TX
19 September 2020

38442369R00108